| DATE DUE | BORROWER'S NAME | ROOM NUMBER |
|---|---|---|
| | | |
| | | |
| | | |
| | | |
| | | |
| | | |
| | | |
| | | |

# *Isaac Asimov*

Twayne's United States Authors Series

Warren French, Editor

*University College of Swansea, Wales*

TUSAS 578

Isaac Asimov.
*Photograph by Kurt Muller*

# *Isaac Asimov*

William F. Touponce

*Indiana University at Indianapolis*

Twayne Publishers • Boston
*A Division of G. K. Hall & Co.*

*Isaac Asimov*
William F. Touponce


Published by Twayne Publishers
A division of G. K. Hall & Co.
70 Lincoln Street
Boston, Massachusetts 02111

Copyediting supervised by India Koopman.
Book production by Janet Z. Reynolds.
Book design by Barbara Anderson.
Typeset by Graphic Sciences Corporation, Cedar Rapids, Iowa.

First published 1991.
10 9 8 7 6 5 4 3 2 1

The paper used in this publication meets the minimum requirements of American National Standard for Information Sciences—Permanence of Paper for Printed Library Materials, ANSI Z39.48-1984. ∞™

Printed and bound in the United States of America.

**Library of Congress Cataloging-in-Publication Data**

Touponce, William F.
Isaac Asimov / William F. Touponce.
p. cm. — (Twayne's United States authors series ; TUSAS 578)
Includes bibliographical references and index.
ISBN 0-8057-7623-0 (alk. paper)
1. Asimov, Isaac, 1920– —Criticism and interpretation.
2. Science fiction, American—History and criticism. I. Title.
II. Series.
PS3551.S5Z88 1991
813′.54—dc20 90-20199
CIP

*To my wife, Chang Ren-Hsiang*

# *Contents*

# *Preface*

In this study I attempt to provide an account of the major works of science fiction by Isaac Asimov. Until recently, these works were organized into two separate series based on two separate sciences—robotics (the robot novels) and psychohistory (the Foundation novels)—with the Galactic Empire novels falling in between. Most critics writing on Asimov have dealt with his works in order of date of publication. But since Asimov has chosen to write both sequels and "prequels" to his two series, linking them together into an integrated vision, a vast fifteen-novel epic of the future, the chronological approach has its limitations—especially if one aims to provide an overview of an entire imaginative universe. As interesting as the circumstances of publication are, and as valid as James Gunn's "criticism in context" approach to Asimov (from which I have gleaned much) may be, I have chosen to approach Asimov in the manner he himself has suggested. That is, this study progresses according to the chronological order of the books in terms of future history, not publication date. It begins with *The End of Eternity,* in which Asimov creates a unique historical time line. The study focuses next on the robot novels, then on the novels set in the early centuries of the Galactic Empire, and finally on the Foundation novels. In all, Asimov's major works represent some twenty thousand years of future history.

The advantage of this approach is obvious: the reader can grasp the basic story of a given novel, as well as that story's role in the development of Asimov's future history, in the same discussion. Throughout the book I not only discuss each novel but also examine the aspects of narrative continuity within it that link it to other narratives of the Asimovian universe. Indeed, giving an account of the enormous narrative work that this future history performs on itself—transforming history and science into myth and legend and back again—is an important aspect of this study. I have been guided by certain advances in the study of narrative, particularly those embodied in Gerard Genette's *Narrative Discourse,*[1] which is so useful in understanding how longer narrative structures are formed.

Although I make use of narratology in this study, however, my primary focus is on Asimovian narrative and how it relates to science—indeed, how it legitimates the rational programs of science, operating for the most part within the paradigms of "normal" science, which thrives on the uninterrupted flow of knowledge and the benefits of progress. I am much indebted to Thomas Kuhn's *The Structure of Scientific Revolutions*[2] and to the writings of Karl Popper for my understanding of how the logic of scientific discovery proceeds and how the history of science has been understood among scientists.

Asimov, the world's most prolific science writer, was trained in a scientific research tradition. Surely this has had as much of an impact on his writing of science fiction as have any of his precursors in the genre. I have sought to uncover, where I could, the narrative connections between his science writing and his career as a science-fiction writer. My primary interest in the insights of Kuhn and Popper concerns what they tell me about the two invented sciences of Asimov, robotics and psychohistory. How do they relate to real sciences? How does the logic of scientific discovery relate to the logic of science-fiction narrative in Asimov? I believe I have found—at least provisionally—some fundamental answers to these questions, which critics have not observed before.

But Asimov has a habit of outdistancing his critics, making their comments outmoded by publishing another book that revises the assumptions of the books that went before. Indeed, as Asimov understands it, that is in part how science proceeds: by questioning hidden assumptions. So perhaps, when dealing with Asimov, it is best to be modest and remember the comment made by Brian Aldiss in his history of science fiction, *Trillion-Year Spree:* "Asimov is the great giant sandworm of science fiction, tunnelling under its arid places. And the critic's job remains that of a small termite, tunnelling under Asimov."[3]

Chapter 1 of the tunnelings that make up this book tells the story of how Asimov became an acknowledged master in the field of science fiction. I have drawn extensively on Asimov's autobiography and on an interview I conducted with him in the summer of 1988, during which I found him to be a genial and humorous man. The bulk of the book is devoted to Asimov's novels, analyzed in the light of narratology and of Kuhn's notion of paradigms that guide scientific research. The final chapter sums up Asimov's reception among critics and touches on his other fiction. The appendix lists the main characters in the Asimovian universe and the novels in which they occur. It should be noted at the outset, however, that in Asimovian fiction, character is little more than a function of, or stand-in for, ideas.

# *Chronology*

1920 Isaac Asimov born 2 January (although birthdate may be as early as 4 October 1919) in Petrovichi, Russia, first child of Judah Asimov and Anna Rachel Asimov (née Berman).

1922 Asimov's sister Manya (Marcia) born 17 June.

1923 Asimov family emigrates to United States and settles in Brooklyn in February.

1928 Becomes U.S. citizen.

1929 Discovers science-fiction magazines and becomes a fan. Brother Stanley born 25 July.

1935 Enters Seth Low Junior College of Columbia University. A letter he writes to *Astounding Stories* is published.

1936 Transfers to the main campus of Columbia University.

1937 Writes more letters to *Astounding*. Begins writing "Cosmic Corkscrew." Reads Gibbon's *The Decline and Fall of the Roman Empire*.

1938 Begins to keep a diary and associates with the Futurians. Takes "Cosmic Corkscrew" to John W. Campbell, Jr., new editor of *Astounding*.

1939 First published story, "Marooned off Vesta," appears in *Amazing Stories;* "Trends" published in *Astounding*. Earns B.S. degree from Columbia and enters graduate school there, majoring in chemistry. Begins writing robot stories. Attends first world science-fiction convention in New York.

1940 "Robbie," published under title "Strange Playfellow" (September *Super Science Stories*), is first story of positronic robot series. In December meeting with Campbell, Asimov works out the Three Laws of Robotics.

1941 Publication of "Nightfall" (September *Astounding*) marks his acceptance as a major figure in science fiction at the age of twenty-one. Publishes two more positronic robot stories: "Reason" and "Liar." Earns M.A. in chemistry.

1942 Begins Foundation series with "Foundation" (May *Astounding*).

"Runaround" (March *Astounding*) is first story in which all three Laws of Robotics are explicitly stated. Suspends studies to work as chemist at U.S. Navy Yard in Philadelphia. Marries Gertrude Blugerman 26 July.

1943 Because of the combined effects of being separated from New York (and Campbell) and receiving a regular paycheck, largely suspends writing.

1944 Publishes two more installments in the Foundation series and another robot story. Reads Toynbee's *A Study of History.*

1945 Publishes first Foundation story to be influenced by Toynbee's thought, "Dead Hand" (April *Astounding*), and "The Mule" (August *Astounding*). Drafted after V-J Day (and released less than a year later).

1946 Returns to studies at Columbia.

1947 Publishes "Little Lost Robot" (March *Astounding*). His robot stories and Foundation series have made him a science-fiction celebrity of the first rank. Attends Philcon (the fifth World Science Fiction Convention, held in Philadelphia) and is interviewed by a reporter for the first time.

1948 Earns Ph.D. and takes up postdoctorate work at Columbia.

1949 Hired as an instructor in biochemistry at Boston University School of Medicine.

1950 In January *Astounding* publishes last of Foundation series, which is left open-ended at Campbell's insistence. Doubleday publishes Asimov's first novel, *Pebble in the Sky.* Gnome Press publishes his first collection, *I, Robot,* for which he writes a framing story about Susan Calvin. His books continue to appear every year. Attends Breadloaf Writers Conference.

1951 *Foundation* published by Gnome Press. Asimov writes an introduction for it ("The Psychohistorians"). *The Stars Like Dust* (novel). Son David born. Promoted to assistant professor.

1952 *The Currents of Space* (novel). Doubleday publishes first Lucky Starr juvenile. First nonfiction book, *Biochemistry and Human Metabolism* (co-author). *Foundation and Empire.* Asimov continues to alternate works of science fiction with nonfiction books and articles, particularly science popularizations.

1953 *Second Foundation.* Begins to seek other markets for his stories beyond Campbell. *The Caves of Steel* serialized in Horace Gold's *Galaxy.*

1954 *The Caves of Steel* (novel).

1955 *The End of Eternity* (novel). *The Martian Way and Other Stories.* Guest of honor at thirteenth annual World Science Fiction Convention in Cleveland. Promoted to associate professor. Daughter Robyn born.

1956 *The Naked Sun* serialized in *Astounding.* Publishes "The Last Question" (in his opinion his best science-fiction story), and "What's in a Name?" (his first straight mystery story) in June *Saint Detective Magazine.* Earns ten dollars for his first paid talk and begins career as popular speaker.

1957 *Earth Is Room Enough* (stories). *The Naked Sun* (novel). Soviet Union launches Sputnik I. Asimov increasingly drawn to nonfiction.

1958 Begins his first monthly science column for *Magazine of Fantasy and Science Fiction.* Leaves full-time teaching for full-time freelance writing. After 1958 publishes no new science-fiction novels until novelization of screenplay for *Fantastic Voyage* (1966) and *The Gods Themselves* (novel, 1972). Writes short science-fiction stories occasionally, but mainly writes nonfiction. "Lastborn" ("The Ugly Little Boy") appears in September *Galaxy. The Death Dealers* (mystery novel).

1959 *Nine Tomorrows* (stories).

1960 *The Intelligent Man's Guide to Science.* Wins critical approval and, for the first time, reviews in national magazines. Nominated for National Book Award.

1962 Edits *The Hugo Winners* (the first of his anthologies), and in it writes the first of the autobiographical comments that will characterize all of his future anthologies and collections. *Words in Genesis.* Wins Boston University's Publication Merit Award.

1963 Awarded Special Hugo by World Science Fiction Convention for his science articles in *Fantasy and Science Fiction.*

1964 *The Rest of the Robots* (stories). Wins James T. Grady medal for science writing in the field of chemistry, given by American Chemical Society. Boston University begins to collect his papers.

1965 Writes humorous articles for *TV Guide* that reach a mass audience.

1966 *Fantastic Voyage* (novelization). Is guest of honor at twenty-fourth

World Science Fiction Convention in Cleveland. Foundation series wins Hugo. Special issue of *Fantasy and Science Fiction* dedicated to Asimov and his work.

1967 Writes two forewords to Harlan Ellison's *Dangerous Visions*. Receives E. E. Smith Memorial Award. Wins Westinghouse–AAAS (American Association for the Advancement of Science) prize for science writing.

1968 *Asimov's Guide to the Bible*, vol. 1. *Asimov's Mysteries.*

1969 *Asimov's Guide to the Bible*, vol. 2. *Nightfall and Other Stories. Opus 100.* Father dies.

1970 *Asimov's Guide to Shakespeare*. Separates from wife and moves back to New York. Receives first honorary degree (Doctor of Science) from Bridgewater State College, Massachusetts.

1971 *The Best New Thing* (children's book). At Breadloaf, gives talk on intolerance.

1972 *The Gods Themselves* (novel). *The Early Asimov* (semiautobiographical collection dealing with science fiction of the 1940s). *Asimov's Annotated Don Juan*. Undergoes thyroidectomy.

1973 Wins Nebula and Hugo awards for *The Gods Themselves*. Divorces first wife and marries Dr. Janet Jeppson.

1974 *Before the Golden Age* (semiautobiographical collection dealing with science fiction of the 1930s). *Asimov's Annotated Paradise Lost. Tales of the Black Widowers.*

1975 *Buy Jupiter and Other Stories* (semiautobiographical collection dealing with science fiction of the 1950s). *Lecherous Limericks.*

1976 *Murder at the ABA* (mystery novel). *The Bicentennial Man and Other Stories. Familiar Poems, Annotated.* First issue of *Isaac Asimov's Science Fiction Magazine.*

1977 "The Bicentennial Man" (novelette) wins Nebula and Hugo awards. Hospitalized with first coronary.

1978 *Limericks: Too Gross.* First issue of *Asimov's SF Adventure Magazine* (suspended after four issues).

1979 *Opus 200. In Memory Yet Green* (autobiography). Promoted to rank of full professor.

1980 *In Joy Still Felt* (autobiography).

1981 *Asimov on Science Fiction* (critical essays).

1982 *Foundation's Edge,* his 262nd book and first novel in ten years, becomes a best-seller.

1983 *The Robots of Dawn* (novel). *The Winds of Change and Other Stories. Foundation's Edge* wins Hugo Award. Asimov undergoes triple coronary bypass operation.

1984 *Opus 300.*

1985 *Robots and Empire* (novel).

1986 *Foundation and Earth* (novel). *Robot Dreams* (collection). *The Alternate Asimovs* (original versions of *Pebble in the Sky* and *The End of Eternity*).

1987 *Fantastic Voyage II: Destination Brain* (novel). Wins Davis Readers Award for "Robot Dreams" (short story). Wins Science Fiction Writers of America Grand Master Award.

1988 *Prelude to Foundation* (novel; opus 379). *Azazel* (collection of fantasy stories). Profiled in *Time* magazine. Appears on television ("Bill Moyers's Journal"). Becomes president of American Humanist Association.

1989 *Asimov's Galaxy* (essays). *Nemesis* (novel).

1990 *Robot Visions* (stories and essays). *Nightfall* (novel; co-authored with Robert Silverberg).

# *Chapter One*
# Life and Intellectual Background

## Rationality and Writing

"To everyone but myself, my life is not at all exciting. It's just a matter of writing, writing, writing."[1] This is the characteristic Asimovian rejoinder to those eagerly hoping to find some key dramatic event in his life, some central obsession perhaps, that would explain the most salient fact about the man and what he regards as most important about himself: his prolificness. Asimov has published over four hundred books, both fiction and nonfiction. He started writing professionally in the 1930s when he was only eighteen years old. During his twenties he coined two new words, one derived from literature, the other from science: *robotics* and *positronic*. Today, at seventy, he shows no signs of slowing down. Despite disclaimers about the growing frailties of old age (Asimov underwent a triple coronary bypass in 1983), he continues to publish books every year, as a glance at the chronology will show. He still devotes at least seven hours a day to working on various projects, and all else—social obligations, entertainment, interviews—comes second. More than anything else in his life, his simple set of priorities, which puts writing above all else, has been the key to his success. As one interviewer noted, the work is both his hunger and his feast.[2]

To most of us, living on a schedule as rigid as Asimov's would seem grueling, and the intense focus on writing would seem to border on neurosis. But for Asimov writing is a source of immense intellectual pleasure. It seems fair to say that no one has written more books on more different subjects: lecherous limericks, mystery novels, the meaning of Greek myths, a commentary on Genesis, a history of the birth of America, mathematics, the sciences (over thirty books on astronomy alone), and science fiction. A recent *Time* magazine profile dubbed him "an incurable explainaholic" who relishes making difficult subjects accessible to the common reader, intent on convincing the world to adopt his vision of scientific rationality.[3] For Asimov, a large part of that vision lies in the belief that scientific truth alone, when sufficiently explained to people, is enough to convince them: "I continue to write books on science and history—and science fiction too—in which I try to explain the world in a natural, rationalist way, with the confident certainty that one has but to do that to cause people to abandon their foolish superstitions."[4] This project of bringing scientific knowledge to the general population is what primarily accounts for his enormous output: scientific knowledge continues to grow, and the forces of darkness and ignorance are, in Asimov's view, never permanently defeated.

Asimov has his darker, more cynical moments when he sees supposedly educated people embrace a wide variety of what he considers to be irrational beliefs. In his discussion of evolution in *Asimov's New Guide to Science* (1984), for example, he rails against the intellectual contradictions inherent in "scientific creationism."[5] And when he feels that science is being attacked, he can respond with caustic remarks. But at heart he is an avowed humanist, tolerant of religious beliefs in others.[6] He views technology and science, wisely used, as beneficent and as the key to human progress. He was, however, vehemently opposed to the Reagan administration's Star Wars initiative, for he believes that nation-states are an outmoded form of government, ill-equipped to meet the global problems (overpopulation, pollution) that we face. If we are to survive as a species, he argues, then we must "begin to look for ways of attaining a rational disarmament and a reasonable form of world government."[7] His general intellectual stance, though, encompasses an ebullient, upbeat view of life that has much in common with that of the philosophers and encyclopedists of the eighteenth century, and all his important works resonate with the spirit of the Enlightenment.[8]

To narrate as much of the story of scientific enlightenment as he can has become his life's project. It is also the way in which he finds significance in his life and influences the world, convincing enough rational people (he hopes) to make a difference. Asimov takes pride in relating the fact that he described in detail the euphoria of a space walk decades before it actually happened, or that a young scientist found the key to a difficult scientific experiment through reading one of his science articles, or that a student was inspired by his robot stories to found a company that now manufactures one-third of all the industrial robots in use (Joseph F. Engelberger, president of Unimation).

The intellectual adventures of Asimov's books are the important "events" of his life, recorded in his massive two-volume autobiography of over half a million words. Although it is more than thirty years since he gave up formal classroom teaching at Boston University (he holds a Ph.D. in biochemistry), Asimov does not regret "no longer being a scientist." On the contrary, he argues that science popularization is necessary to the scientist. Indeed, he regards it as the first duty of any scientist not engaged in research. So in this sense, for Asimov, writing is the way to remain a working scientist. And while it is certainly true that there is not much drama in sitting in front of a typewriter for most of one's life, Asimov—through his books and lectures—has reached a far larger audience in more fields than almost any author in history.

Asimov's commitment to rationality and writing of course implies a style. In his writing, he aims for clarity and transparency. Whether we observe it in the context of science popularization or science fiction, the typical Asimovian sentence subordinates everything to clarity of meaning. He has mastered the difficult trick of making the words seem unnoticeable so that the concepts they bear can shine through. So intent is he on this illusion of transparency in writing that he denies even having, or deliberately trying to create, a literary or public persona—a concept that tends to negate the writer's capacity to speak in his own voice. Yet in his many first-person introductions and prefaces to his works, and especially in his autobiography, he certainly does play with his public's image of him as a genius.[9] Although at a first glance Asimov's autobiography may strike us as a kind of daunting laundry list, Asimov is able to keep us interested—indeed, charmed and somewhat off balance—by means of his personable style and the humorous anecdotes he tells. This style is a savvy mixture of cheerful self-appreciation—a celebration of his considerable and polymath intelligence—and self-denigration:

> I love to talk about myself, as I have no secrets. But I make no pretense that I haven't got my weaknesses. I'll tell you one little story about my autobiography. Someone said to me that they found it really fascinating to read. And I said, "But didn't you notice that nothing ever happens in it?" And he replied: "Oh yeah, I noticed, but I didn't care!" I've had the quietest conceivable life, you see. In my science essays for *Fantasy and Science Fiction,* of which I have just written my three hundred and sixty-fourth, I always—or at least all except for the very first few—start off with a personal anecdote, invariably true. I polish them up sometimes so that in the telling they glitter a little more than real life, but they are essentially true.[10]

As might be supposed, Asimov's characteristic mode of writing is storytelling, or narration. He has an abiding love for history and for historical explanation (he claims to have read Gibbon's *The Decline and Fall of the Roman Empire* at least twice). Very early in his writing career he realized that almost anything could be taught or understood historically, and that most areas of human knowledge could profitably be arranged for study along a continuum, from the simple to the complex. In fact, many of his informational books do have an underlying narrative structure, although at first glance they may appear to be arranged solely according to topic, category, location, or some other criterion. This is true of *The Intelligent Man's Guide to Science* (1960), the book that made his reputation as a science popularizer. It is undoubtedly his single most important nonfictional work, if only because it takes almost all of science as its field of review. The *Guide* begins with the universe as a whole and works its way inward in narrowing circles, from the physical sciences through the biological sciences, until it reaches the human mind. But the apparent organization is underlaid by a more fundamental historical perspective.

In his autobiography, Asimov tells us that his plan for the *Guide* "made it natural to present the subject in historical perspective. . . . it gave me the chance to present a logical unfolding of a field of knowledge, to make an exciting story out of it, with the scientist as hero and with ignorance as the villain."[11] Thus it is important to recognize that these narrative structures of enlightenment—providing knowledge through narrative—play the most important unifying roles in Asimov's enormous body of work and serve to legitimize science in our society as well.

While it would be instructive to examine more of Asimov's science books, the one example given will have to suffice. Besides, Asimov thinks of himself primarily as a science-fiction writer. He started out as a science-fiction writer, and it is as such that he wants to continue to be identified. In his autobiography Asimov self-consciously talks about himself as a science-fiction writer who has helped, in his career, to chronicle the history of modern science fiction. I have necessarily drawn upon this "reference guide to Asimov" (as he describes it)—as well as upon my 1988 interview with him—in preparing this chapter's account of his life.

## The Autobiography: Making Reference

Asimov planned his autobiography as a complete and very personal literary reference work in which his fans could discover almost any detail about every piece of fiction he has written. The first volume, *In Memory Yet Green* (1979), covers the first thirty-four years of his life (1920–54); the second, *In Joy Still Felt* (1980), covers the next twenty-four (1954–78).

Asimov has indicated that he also wrote his autobiography as an experiment. That is, he endeavored to make it absolutely chronological: "I did not skip here and there across the years in order to make some point. I did not make use of foreshadowings. At every point in the autobiography, I tried to reveal no more than I knew at that moment in my life. The reader knows only what I know and lives my life along with me."[12] On occasion he does, however, look backward, as an older and wiser man, on the experiences of his youth—and when he does, an interesting duality arises between the narrating self and the experiencing self (as evidenced by his current perspective on experiences during his military service, touched on in the next section of this chapter). Also, Asimov thought he should record "every piece of egregious Asimovian stupidity" he could remember, in order to counter his reputation for universal wisdom.

This partial self-debunking makes the book all the more engaging to read, but Asimov is no Proustian narrator. The book is mostly a factual account of his life. The narrative comes primarily from his excellent memory and a diary that he has kept since 1938. He omitted all philosophical rumination, leaving it up to each reader to supply his or her own interpretation of the facts. A third volume is planned—*The Scenes of Life* is the working title—although Asimov has yet to find the time to finish it.

Isaac Asimov was born to middle-class Jewish parents on 2 January 1920 in Petrovichi, Russia, part of the Smolensk district of the U.S.S.R. (He speaks and understands both English and Yiddish with equal ease.) He remembers his father as someone who loved to tell him stories and parables designed to improve his mind and spirit, but his mother as a terrible-tempered woman who did not follow the same philosophy of child-rearing. It was she who often administered corporal punishment to the young Asimov, together with lectures that made use of the extensive Yiddish vocabulary of derogatory terms.

In 1923 the Asimovs (now including Asimov's sister, who had been born the previous year) emigrated to America, settling in New York City's borough of Brooklyn, where Isaac was to spend his formative years. One of Asimov's earliest memories of America is an incredible longing to understand what the various signs he saw all about him meant. He seems to have decoded written English entirely by himself, since his parents were functionally illiterate in the new tongue (his account of how he did this is one of the most fascinating episodes in the book). In effect, Asimov went to segregated public schools throughout his childhood, since the student body was always heavily Jewish. After ordinary school was over, he attended Hebrew school, at least until the family moved again. He never really mastered the Hebrew language. At home he was brought up with next to no religious training. He remembers his father loading him down with Talmudic aphorisms about life and how to conduct himself, but the elder Asimov was not Orthodox, so Isaac was a freethinker from the start and never had to break with a religious past.

The Asimov family owned and operated a series of candy stores in Brooklyn. Asimov claims that he was "orphaned" by these stores because he never interacted with any of his family members in any other context. This may be an exaggeration, but there is no doubt that his duties in the store kept him from enjoying a full social life. Furthermore, his father's imputations about laziness leading to a bad end seem to have shaped Asimov's character permanently: "I am forever and always in the candy store, and the work must be done."[13] More than anything else, Asimov claims, it is the memory of his father that has made him so prolific.

On the other hand though, there were compensations. The candy store had magazines, including pulp magazines: the detective stories, the Westerns, the adventures, and most importantly for Asimov, the science-fiction magazines. In 1929 he began reading such science-fiction magazines as *Amazing Stories* and became a fan. The insular life of the candy store attracted him further into the world of literature, and he became an assiduous librarygoer. His early bookreading was primarily in nineteenth-century British fiction: "I became a spiritual Englishman and a conscious Anglophile."[14] To this day, a great deal of Asimovian character dialogue is studded with British phrases. Perhaps it is part of this felt spiritual Englishness that Asimov lays claim to certain eccentricities—love of cemeteries, for instance—conventionally associated with the British romantics. (He also sports a pair of voluminous Victorian sideburns.)

As for most serious twentieth-century fiction, Asimov asserts that it is quite beyond him. He never discovered twentieth-century realism—has never read Hemingway or Fitzgerald or Joyce or Kafka—although he has read a great deal of historical fiction and history. Of all the twentieth-century writers, he rereads primarily Agatha Christie and P. G. Wodehouse. Mystery and humor are, of course, two genres in which he himself likes to work (see *Asimov's Mysteries*).

In 1930 Asimov entered junior high school, where he began to retell stories from the science-fiction magazines to his classmates. A year later he attempted his first fiction writing by imitating boys' series books. When Asimov was thirteen, he was not bar mitzvahed—but according to him, he was a confirmed atheist by then anyway. Around that time, the precocious boy's political views began to take shape. When Franklin D. Roosevelt won the presidential election in 1932, Asimov began a lifelong commitment to liberal democratic politics. At Boys High School of Brooklyn in 1934 he published his first nonprofessional story, "Little

Brothers"—a humorous essay after the style of Robert Benchley—in the school's literary semiannual.

The next year he entered Seth Low Junior College, an undergraduate college of Columbia University. For the first time he tried to write science fiction. What emerged was an epic story about a catastrophe that destroyed photosynthesis on Earth. Unfortunately, the manuscript did not survive the 1940s, but Asimov can still remember parts of it. What did survive was a letter he wrote to *Astounding Stories,* which today makes him a member of an organization known as First Fandom, whose membership consists of those who had been active fans of science fiction prior to 1938. Actually, Asimov was never a very active fan, although he did briefly join the Futurians. One of that organization's other members was Frederik Pohl, who was later to operate sometimes as an agent for Asimov, who became a professional writer at nineteen.

In 1936 he transferred to the main campus of Columbia University, where he switched his major from biology to chemistry. Because of an aversion to dissection, he began to doubt whether he wanted to go to medical school as his parents wished. During the next two years his growing interest in historical fiction intensified his interest in history itself. He read H. G. Wells's *Outline of History* and Gibbon's *Decline and Fall of the Roman Empire.* He continued to read science fiction avidly and wrote more letters to *Astounding.* In June 1938 he finished his first piece of fiction ever completed with a view toward publication. A story entitled "Cosmic Corkscrew," it dealt with a concept of time as a helical structure. He delivered the story personally to John W. Campbell, Jr., editor of *Astounding,* who impressed Asimov immensely. Campbell rejected the story, and eventually the manuscript was lost, but Asimov had begun a professional relationship with a man who was to be a greater influence on him than anyone but his father.

From mid-1938 on, Asimov began to write more and more stories, submitting them to various science-fiction pulp magazines, but always hoping to break into Campbell's *Astounding,* which had the most prestige. His first published story, "Marooned off Vesta," appeared in a 1939 issue of *Amazing Stories,* a magazine that Hugo Gernsback had founded. Among Asimov's other early stories was "Strange Playfellow" (later retitled "Robbie"), which concerned a sympathetic and noble robot that served as a nursemaid for a little girl. The first of his positronic robot stories, it was eventually published in 1940 in *Super Science Stories.* Although Campbell had rejected "Strange Playfellow," he accepted another story, "Trends." As an editor, Campbell was looking for stories that involved specifically described scientific extrapolation, and "Trends," about social resistance to space flight, took shape as a story very much in Campbell's mold. After eight consecutive rejections and revisions, he finally accepted it for publication (it is now collected in *The Early Asimov*). Asimov regards this story as his first significant publication.

The summer of 1939 had been one of doubt and uncertainty for Asimov. He had graduated from Columbia and obtained his Bachelor of Science degree in chemistry but had not been accepted into medical school. What is more, Columbia initially seemed unwilling to take him for graduate work in chemistry. But by agreeing to double up on required courses in his first year of graduate study, he convinced the admissions board that he was seriously interested in chemistry. That summer Asimov attended The First World Science Fiction Convention in New York, where he met many luminaries in the science fiction field—illustrators, writers, and editors—and gave a brief speech.

For the next eleven years of his literary career, Asimov wrote nothing but magazine science fiction. In December 1940 he met with Campbell and worked out the Three Laws of Robotics, which have governed the production of his robot stories ever since. Asimov was tired of the typical robot story, in which the robot turned against its maker. He wanted robots that were engineered to be safe, just as other human-made tools were. But aside from that, Asimov leaned toward the production of more robot stories for Campbell because of a ideological quirk of Campbell's that bordered on overt racism. Campbell wanted white Europeans to win out over extraterrestrials in the stories he published. In Asimov's view, this was an unfortunate reflection of the ongoing historical situation:

> John Campbell always believed that humans would win out. He belonged to the period when it was taken for granted that northwest European human beings were the pinnacle of civilization in ability, intellect, and so on. And when he wrote about numerous intelligent species, human beings represented the northwest Europeans of the Galaxy! I ran into trouble when I tried to write stories like that too. In 1940 I wrote a story called "Homo Sol" [in *The Early Asimov;* the story, still not as Asimov originally wrote it, reflects some of Campbell's changes], which was the second one of my stories that he printed, in which I had different intelligences on every planet. And I didn't *want* to make it look as though the Earthmen were the cream of the Galaxy. It was 1940, for goodness' sake—World War II was on and Hitler looked as though he was going to win. Northwest Europeans were slaughtering the Jews—and I'm Jewish—and I wasn't intent on boosting the Aryan myth. And he insisted. So I decided to write stories in which there were no aliens. And that way I could sell him stories without violating my own feelings. So I invented the all-human Galaxy. . . . (1988 interview)

In other words, in the robot stories Asimov didn't mind making human beings superior to robots, and writing them did not involve him in a hassle with Campbell.

These stories, with which Asimov made his first true mark on science fiction, were then the end product of a "peculiar symbiotic relation" with Campbell, as was another story he wrote for Campbell at the time, "Nightfall," which many consider to be the best science-fiction story of all time. As a matter of fact, near the end of the story, which explores the reactions of human beings on a planet where the night sky appears once in a thousand years, Campbell inserted a paragraph of his own (Asimov believes that it seriously flaws the story). Asimov does not consider "Nightfall" to be among his best stories, but after it he never wrote another science-fiction story that remained unpublished, so it constitutes a milestone in his development as a science-fiction author. Certainly, after the publication of "Nightfall" in the September 1941 issue of *Astounding* (which featured a front-cover illustration of the story), Asimov was accepted as a major figure in the field at the age of twenty-one.

## From the Science of History to the History of Science

The next big step in the development of Asimov's career was the Foundation series. In August of 1941 Asimov got the idea of writing a future-historical story about the fall of a Galactic Empire, suggested in part by Gibbon's *Decline and Fall.* Although Asimov was thinking about a novelette, Campbell wanted an open-ended series of stories, all fitting into a particular future history involving the fall of the First Galactic Empire, an interregnum, and the rise of the Second Galactic Empire. As Asimov clearly indicates in the passage quoted earlier, it was his fixed intention to prevent Campbell from foisting on him his notions of the superiority and inferiority of races. The surest way to do this in the context of a Galactic Empire was to write about an all-human Galaxy, a concept that apparently had not yet been used in science fiction. Asimov is often given credit for establishing this convention.

Asimov worked on the series until 1950, eventually publishing eight separate stories that were later shaped into three novels that subsequently became the Foundation Trilogy (although they are in fact neither novels nor a trilogy). At least one of the stories, "Dead Hand" (*Astounding,* April 1945), was influenced by Toynbee's *A Study of History,* which tells of recurring cycles in the historical process. But the Foundation Trilogy novels are most famous for their postulation of a science of history, psychohistory—"the prediction of future trends in history through mathematical analysis"—that would reduce the intervening years of barbarism from thirty thousand years to one thousand. Just as Asimov had earlier predicted the use of assembly-line robotics and narrated the theory of the positronic brain with his robot stories (of which he was also writing more throughout the 1940s), he now narrated scientific theory in another, more sweeping, historical context. By 1947, largely because of these two invented sciences, Asimov had become a science-fiction celebrity of the first rank.

His personal life was also changing rapidly during the early 1940s. He had earned his M.A. in chemistry in 1941, but because of the war he had to suspend his studies to be a junior research chemist at the U.S. Navy Yard in Philadelphia, where L. Sprague de Camp and Robert Heinlein (whom Asimov accepted as the best science-fiction writer in the field) also worked. It was a permanent break with the candy store after nearly sixteen years of working in it, as well as his first real separation from his parents. He even stopped reading science-fiction magazines for the first time in thirteen years. During this period he also met and married his first wife, Gertrude Blugerman, a native of Toronto, Canada, who had moved with her family to New York in 1936. Her father was a businessman who owned a paper box manufacturing company. She had completed the equivalent of the college freshman year in education and respected Asimov's intelligence. They promptly set up housekeeping in Philadelphia.

Asimov was not drafted until after the victory over Japan. His military service was uneventful, except for a personal turning point that he experienced during his stay in Hawaii. After reflecting on an incident in which he tried to educate some of his fellow soldiers about the workings of the atom bomb, Asimov realized that his insistence on displaying his intelligence and learning to others wearied people and made them dislike him. This insight inspired a shift in his attitude toward others that enabled him to transform himself from a "generally disliked know-it-all" to a generally liked "genial nonpusher," as he was to describe himself in his later years. Incidentally, as Asimov has often pointed out, it was primarily because of the atom bomb that it became difficult for the general public to think of science fiction as childish and silly anymore. Writers in the field felt that there were great days ahead, especially when the market for science-fiction novels opened in the 1950s.

In 1946 Asimov returned to his studies at Columbia, where he finished his Ph.D. in 1948. A year later he was hired as an instructor in biochemistry at Boston University School of Medicine. He accepted the teaching job largely because he felt insecure about his writing career. At the time, he could not see himself making a living as a writer. He wondered if he might be a one-editor writer: as he had always discussed his stories with Campbell, he could not help thinking that much of their success was due to Campbell. Nevertheless, tired of the Foundation/robot rut and alienated by Campbell's increasing enthusiasm for pseudoscience (dianetics, psionic powers), Asimov decided to reach out to other editors in the field, especially to Horace Gold, editor of *Galaxy.* In 1952 Gold wanted a robot novel from Asimov and suggested a murder mystery in which a detective solves the crime with a robot partner. Gold wanted one condition of the story to be that if the detective didn't solve the crime, he would be replaced by the robot. When Asimov wrote *The Caves of Steel* (which Gold serialized in *Galaxy* in 1953), he tried to resist the idea of robots replacing human beings, but in the end Gold pushed him into using it—just as Campbell, ten years earlier, had forced him to write on the idea of symbolic logic:

> John Campbell, you have to understand, had his own ideas. He would force them on writers. And the symbolic logic bit in "Foundation" [*Astounding,* May 1942; Part I of *Foundation*] was not the only case. He insisted on my sticking in the stuff about religion in "Bridle and Saddle" [*Astounding,* June 1942; Part II of *Foundation*], which I didn't want to do. And his final bit was to insist on the story of the mutant in "The Mule" [*Astounding,* August 1945; Part II of *Foundation and Empire*]. That worked fine; he was right, there. But in many cases he was not right, at least from my viewpoint. And as time went on I became less and less amenable to this sort of thing. By the 1950s it was very rare that an editor could get me to make a major change. The one exception was in "The Ugly Little Boy" [published as "Lastborn" in *Galaxy,* September 1958], when Horace Gold objected to what I had written and asked me, knowing my quick temper, to make any *one* of three changes he suggested. . . . On thinking it over, I realized he was "righter" than he ever presented himself to be. I was completely wrong . . . but in other cases I refused to make changes for him. (1988 interview)

Asimov was quite annoyed with Gold's forced insertion of the U.S. Constitution as a plot element into his second novel, *The Stars Like Dust* (1951). (Doubleday had published his first science-fiction novel, *Pebble in the Sky,* in 1950.) But with the publication of *The Caves of Steel* in book form (1954), Asimov reached, in his own estimation, the peak of his direct and spare writing style. He records that he was enormously pleased with the book, and he still regards it as an almost perfect fusion of two genres, mystery and science fiction. Yet by 1954 Asimov had also reached a certain limit in his writing because it was confined to the specialized world of biochemistry (he had coauthored a textbook on the subject in 1952) and science fiction. He thought he could perhaps do better than *I, Robot* (1950) or the Foundation series, but not much better. Although *The End of Eternity* (1955) was (and still is) considered one of the best "ludic," or playful, time-travel stories, Asimov was left unsatisfied. How could he move out of his specialized world and reach a larger and more remunerative audience?

The answer, of course, lay in nonfiction writing, and particularly in science popularization. In 1957 the Soviet Union launched Sputnik I, revealing a large gap between our country and theirs in terms of science education. From this point onward, it was science that chiefly interested Asimov. Never again was science fiction to form the main portion of his output. In 1958 Asimov began a monthly science column for the *Magazine of Fantasy and Science Fiction* that continues to this day. Many collections of his science essays have stemmed from this source. In fact, Asimov was awarded a Special Hugo in 1963 for his science articles. Yet the break with science fiction was neither sudden nor entirely complete. During the sixties and seventies, about eighty percent of his output was nonfiction, including such books as *The Wellsprings of Life* (1961), *The Universe* (1966), and *Life and Time* (1978), but nonetheless he managed to publish well over a hundred stories. He continued to publish collections of stories, such as *Nine Tomorrows* (1959) and *The Rest of the Robots* (1964), but wrote no new novels until *The Gods Themselves* (1972), which won him both a Hugo and a Nebula Award.

But in 1960 Asimov published the book that led to his recognition as a major figure in the field of science writing: *The Intelligent Man's Guide to Science* (now *Asimov's New Guide to Science*). Judging from the index to the autobiography, Asimov discusses this book, in its various editions, more than any of his others. Actually, the book has been nominated for a National Book Award and has been printed in four editions. Asimov claims that he liked each edition better than the one before it, and says he thinks the newest edition (1984) is "a terrific book." The only thing that bothers him about it is that sooner or later the publisher, Basic Books, is going to ask for a fifth edition:

Unfortunately, with each edition I get older and feebler [*laughter*]. I got in [a discussion of] superconductivity, but only the "old-fashioned" kind. I didn't get in the so-called warm superconductivity. Naturally, I didn't get in the new supernova, and I didn't get in the flights past Uranus. And I didn't get in the shuttle disaster—everything since 1984, and that's four years now. So they're going to ask [for another updated volume]. I also have the *Asimov's Biographical Encyclopedia of Science and Technology,* which is now in its third edition. The first edition contained about a thousand biographies of scientists; the second upped it to twelve hundred; the third and present edition has fifteen hundred. If there's a fourth edition I'm going to push for two thousand, but . . . I may not have the strength to do it. Oh dear! (1988 interview)

The "feebleness" to which Asimov refers is related to his heart problems. In 1977 Asimov had to be hospitalized after a heart attack. The attack left him plagued with angina pectoris, which worsened rapidly in 1983. Asimov decided that he was not long for this world unless he took advantage of modern medicine, so on 13 December 1983 he underwent a triple coronary bypass operation: "I came through it with flying colors. That's four and a half years ago, and I feel fine. No angina" (1988 interview). According to a *Time* magazine profile, Asimov's manners and habits changed overnight. Although he had a great appetite for high-cholesterol foods and no taste for exercise, he totally altered his diet and bought an exercise machine that demanded the efforts of cross-country skiing. Week by week he worked himself into shape and dropped fifty pounds: "Well, at my maximum weight, at the age of forty-four, I weighed 210 pounds. I worked my way down to 180 pounds . . . and then I worked my way down to 160. . . . I [had] started working my way down when I had the angina—and believe me, that was a good push—but by the time I finished my triple bypass I was down to 160. That's fifty pounds less than my maximum, and I've stayed at 160 ever since" (1988 interview). To some readers these facts may seem trivial, but they signal essentially the way in which Asimov has chosen to define himself. His talking style is direct, leisurely, and personal, allowing him to joke about matters as serious as a heart attack.

Other than the heart attack, Asimov's life has been, with few exceptions, relatively calm. He has, of course, won many of science fiction's top awards; I have chosen to mention these in the chronology and in the last chapter, on Asimov's reputation. In 1951, at about the same time as he was working on his biochemistry textbook, a son, David, was born. Four years later came a daughter, Robyn. Asimov seems to have been a doting—although, because of his work, timebound—father. Even his divorce in 1973 was without much rancor (Asimov dutifully records his infidelities for his fans). He soon married Janet Jeppson, a psychiatrist, whom he had met at a science-fiction convention, and settled in Manhattan, where he has pursued his freelance career ever since. He continues to publish primarily nonfiction books—

including commentaries on, and annotations of, the works of such major authors as Shakespeare, Byron, and Milton—broadening his interests at an increasing pace. By his own count, in the decade from 1950 to 1960 he wrote 32 books. From 1960 to 1970 he wrote 70 books, from 1970 to 1980 he wrote 109, and in the past decade he wrote 192.

## From Robots to Empire: Asimov's Return to Science Fiction

Asimov returned to the world of science fiction in 1982 with *Foundation's Edge,* a novel-length sequel to the classic Foundation series, which had been left open-ended (at Campbell's insistence) over thirty years previously. Part of the book was featured in a special issue of *Isaac Asimov's Science Fiction Magazine* (December 1982), with commentaries by Arthur C. Clarke, Larry Niven, Frederik Pohl, Harlan Ellison, and others. Unquestionably, it was the science-fiction publishing event of the year; it was on the *New York Times* best-seller list for 25 weeks and won a Hugo award. Asimov followed up this success with *The Robots of Dawn,* a sequel to the robot novels. His publisher, Doubleday, had wanted another book in the Foundation series, but Asimov had demurred:

> I had written *Foundation's Edge* without any thought as to what {would come} next. I wanted to give myself just a little breathing time. Besides which, I had originally . . . planned a trilogy . . . of my robot novels. I had started that . . . in 1958 [the working title had been *The Bounds of Infinity*], but had gotten interested in doing nonfiction, so I let it go. And now I felt that since *Foundation's Edge* was so successful—and I hadn't thought it would be—writing another book didn't seem to bother the readers. So I wrote *The Robots of Dawn.* (from 1988 interview)

The robot novels and the Foundation series were not originally related to each other. Indeed, no robots existed in the Galactic Empire, which was set thousand of years in the future (the robot novels are set in Earth's twenty-first century). But in *Foundation's Edge* (1982) Asimov made a point of referring to his non-Foundation novels (*The End of Eternity*), indicating how they might fit into the Foundation universe. He also mentioned robots for the first time. In creating the narrative world of *The Robots of Dawn* (1983), however, Asimov embarked on a course that would change his entire imaginative universe: "I amused myself by letting the plot serve the function of pointing the Lije Baley universe in the direction of the Foundation universe." In *Robots and Empire* (1985), Asimov further linked the two series by having a robot, Giskard—unbeknownst to mankind—lay the groundwork for the science of psychohistory. *Foundation and Earth* (1986) works at the far end of the Asimovian universe, when Earth, the robots, and their true intentions are finally (re)discovered. And *Prelude to Foundation* (1988) works the middle ground (although it could be called a "prequel" to the Foundation series). Asimov's 379th book, it tells the story of Hari Seldon's development of psychohistory with the help of the robot R. Daneel Olivaw, who has survived through the centuries of mankind's Galactic Empire.

The main purpose of what follows is to lead the reader through this interconnected Asimovian universe. With the help of narratology, the so-called science of narrative, we will track Asimov, first as he narrates the story of two sciences—a normal one, robotics, and an extraordinary one, psychohistory—and then as he finally weaves them both together into a single, though perhaps not entirely consistent, imaginative vision of the future. This interweaving creates many levels of knowledge and knowledge effects. Depending on where we are, we may be at the bottom of an information blackout (the early universe), or we may know more than do the characters themselves (generally the case in the later books).

As Asimov's imaginative world expanded, it also folded back on itself, transforming history into myth and legend. In fact, we can discern two levels of narrative that constantly play off of each other, creating the cognitive effects that are a main feature of science fiction. Certain narrative forms, such as myth, legend, and history are much more the substance of this vision in later volumes than is any putative science. Indeed, the story that Asimov seems to be telling over and over again is that historical and scientific truth degenerate into myth and legend. But as a narrator engaged in the project of enlightenment, he arranges to have his characters (especially Janov Pelorat, the historian of *Foundation's Edge* and *Foundation and Earth,* discussed in chapter 6) extract the kernel of truth from these (self-created) myths and legends. What finally emerges at the far end of the Asimovian universe is a shift from first-order "natural" narrative—a legend or myth that usually contains a secret or veiled truth—to narrative on a higher plane of understanding, where the story yields its true (e.g., scientific, and therefore rational) significance.[15] And it is largely through this shift of planes that he creates the cognitive effect of science fiction.

# *Chapter Two*
# *The End of Eternity*

## Eternity and Empire

It is instructive to compare the original version of *The End of Eternity* (1955), recently made available in *The Alternate Asimovs* (1986), with the published version.[1] It makes clear how much Asimov reworked the story to make it consistent with his future history, a project he must have envisaged as early as the mid-1950s. At any rate, in 1953 Asimov began a novelette based on a time-travel idea that had occurred to him while browsing back issues of *Time* magazine. The idea involved one of the classic motifs of the time-travel story: a time loop. A time loop is a kind of circular causal structure in which effects may precede their causes. Many science-fiction stories are based on it, including the popular film *Back to the Future* (1985), in which a young man travels to the past and inadvertently replaces his father as the object of his then-unmarried mother's romantic interest. In this comic story, the young man trys to avoid replacing his father, for the obvious reason that otherwise he might never be born. In effect, he has to ensure his own conception. Thus the time loop, as the backbone of a work's causal structure, is inherently paradoxical, but still more logical than the far looser motif of journeys in time per se.[2]

Asimov took the basic time-loop structure and further developed it by supposing that in the future it will be scientifically possible to live outside of time. He then postulated a technocratic group of reality manipulators—a "mental aristocracy" of "tempocrats"—the Eternals. They live out their lives in Eternity, entering into time to effect certain drastic changes that they believe are for the benefit of most humans, but that only they remember having taken place. After telling the story of how Eternity was established and had its roots in time, Asimov then works out how its foundations might be threatened with destruction. It turns out that the invention of the Temporal Field that allows Eternity to exist is itself dependent on a time paradox. Asimov has the main character discover that in founding the new science, its inventor used equations that were not derived until three centuries later, which means that he had help from the future. Eternity knows about this strange paradox in both versions of *The End of Eternity* and in both versions tries to rationalize it by sending an Eternal back in time to found the science. That Eternal is the very man who (unbeknownst to himself) was supposed to have founded the science of time travel in an earlier century. The complication in the plot arises when he is marooned in the wrong century by the misguided and guilty actions of one opposed to the system of Eternity. How can he send a needed (and necessarily concealed) message to the future so that he can be rescued?

If the message were sent by means of an advertisement in a magazine (an idea that came to Asimov when he was perusing the old issues of *Time*), it would then presumably already exist in the archives of the future. For those searching for the lost time-traveler, it would be a matter of finding the advertisement, decoding the message, and locating him. He could then be sent to the proper century to found the science on which his journey had been based. Thus, the invention of the Temporal Field (which makes existence outside of time and the Eternals possible) and the theory behind it could oscillate in time, just as a pendulum oscillates in space, in ever-renewed, perhaps eternal, cycles. In a sense, this is the foundation of the science of Eternity. Asimov is clearly playing with the commonly accepted notion that sciences are founded on a bedrock of positive knowledge.

By February 1954 Asimov had shaped this basic plot of communication across time into a dense twenty-five-thousand-word novelette, which he submitted to Horace Gold of *Galaxy* magazine. Gold rejected the story, and Asimov realized that he had a "dehydrated novel" on his hands. But instead of diluting the story, he added incidents and complications, crafting it into a novel that he tried to make consistent with the rise and fall of his Galactic Empire. For the novel to be consistent with his future history, however, Eternity had to be not just threatened but also destroyed—because in the novelette, the Eternals did not allow space travel to develop until many thousands of centuries in the future. This time line would have made Asimov's Galactic Empire impossible because (as he makes clear in *The End of Eternity*) aliens have conquered the Galaxy by the time man ventures forth to explore it, and mankind's exploration is thus in effect foreclosed. Furthermore, the novelette indicates that three-quarters of all the "quantum changes" made by the Eternals were necessitated by their desire to wipe out the development of fission and fusion bombs without crippling nuclear science. Yet the Earth of the Galactic Empire novels—*The Stars, Like Dust* (1951), *The Currents of Space* (1952), and *Pebble in the Sky* (1950)—has a radioactive crust, a dystopian condition that the Eternals would never have allowed to remain unchanged. And so Asimov chose to destroy Eternity and to allow for Infinity, or the current time line that emerges at the end of the novel—a time line that is basically our own one of early nuclear power, space flight, and galactic expansion.

Asimov himself considers the book underappreciated, unfairly drowned out by his Foundation and Robot novels. In its playful inventiveness and display of temporal paradoxes—for it does not try cleverly to hide them, as some time-travel stories do—*The End of Eternity* is certainly one of Asimov's best novels. In this chapter I will thoroughly examine the book in the light of narratology, employing that discipline's innovative techniques for studying the ordering of time in narrative.[3] Through this analysis, perhaps, we can get beyond the contention of some critics that Asimov's works of science fiction lack adequate characterization and focus on a more interesting issue: how Asimov gives his paradoxical ideas narrative form.

## Asimovian Anachronies

Most narratologic theory presupposes a basic distinction between two levels of narrative: a level of absolute, chronological events and a level of how we learn about those events. The mystery story, for example, seldom if ever proceeds in a chronological manner. In fact, it usually works backward in time, along with the detective, from the last chronological event (the discovery of a dead body) through a reconstruction of who committed the murder and why. Asimov's science-fiction mystery novel *The Caves of Steel* (1954) unfolds in precisely this manner; the identity of the murderer is not revealed until the last pages. Learning about the events in reverse chronological order creates suspense in the reader and invites him or her to form hypotheses and make inferences.

Narratologists have various terms for the two levels of narrative but sometimes consider just one level to be the real object of investigation. Actually, the two levels interact and must be studied together for an adequate understanding of what happens when we read a narrative. In most narratives—unless we are given an absolute chronology of events, or a time line—the story (which is what we will call the first level) has to be derived through a set of inferences based on signs given in the discourse (the second level).

So the story is what we understand through a set of inferences we make about the bare chronology of events, and also about cause and effect. The discourse enables us to learn about those events. Narratologists have theorized that the discourse level of a narrative text composes story events according to certain specifiable principles that relate discourse to story. Of primary importance, of course, is the concept of time, which embodies at least three aspects: order, duration, and frequency.[4] As might be supposed, order has to do with the construction of events in sequence. As mentioned earlier, seldom in narrative is there an exact coincidence between the two levels.

Most Asimovian narrative—including *The End of Eternity*—makes extensive use of temporal duality, especially flashbacks, or the narrating of story events at a point in the text after chronologically later events have been told. In such instances the narration returns to a past point in the story. We also find the opposite technique, foreshadowing, which is the narration of a story event at a point before chronologically earlier events have been mentioned. The narration takes a journey into the future of the story. Asimov tends to use this device sparingly, however, for the obvious reason that it tends to destroy the suspense on which his popular narratives thrive. In order to avoid the cinematic and visual connotations of the terms *flashback* and *foreshadowing,* narratologists such as Gerard Genette have coined the terms *analepsis* and *prolepsis* for the two main types of discordance (*anachronies,* to use Genette's term) between story order and discourse order. Besides, the term *foreshadowing* implies a kind of symbolic effect that we do not intend here. In a pure prolepsis, the reader is presented with a future event before its time and recognizes it as such, whereas foreshadowing is usually recognized in retrospect.

It has to be understood that anachronies extend throughout the Asimovian universe. So what may appear as an "external heterodiegetic prolepsis" (i.e., the narration of a future event that is to occur after the end point of the first narrative and that refers to another character, event, or story line in the Asimovian universe) in *The End of Eternity* may in the last analysis be internal to another story line. For example, the end of *The End of Eternity,* which occurs in 1932 (when Asimov was twelve) establishes a time line in which the first atomic bomb is exploded in 1945, in which the Earth will probably become mostly radioactive, and so on—all of which ties the book into the larger narrative framework and continuity of Asimov's future history. In effect, it forms a reference point from which to understand the anachronies of the Asimovian universe. This embedding or subordination of one story in or to another may radically alter the cognitive status of the story as well. Hence, what is the story of the development of a science in *The End of Eternity* becomes myth in *Foundation's Edge.*

Duration has to do with how long a period of discourse time is given to a story event. There are three basic techniques of using duration in narrative: more or less equalizing periods of discourse (as in dialog), expanding discourse (as when an event that may take only a minute in the story is given several pages in the text), or reducing and compressing discourse (this includes ellipsis). In Asimov's famous short story, "The Last Question" (1956; collected in *Nine Tomorrows,* 1959), we find extraordinary compression of story time: "The stars and Galaxies died and snuffed out, and space grew black after ten trillion years of running down."[5] Ten trillion years are covered in one sentence. Apart from a few minor analepses, the narrative of this story observes a strict linear and chronological order.

Frequency involves the number of times a story event appears on the discourse level, and in what manner (i.e., recounted, mentioned by a character, or enacted). The numerical possibilities are limited and can be tabulated easily. An event is either enacted or recounted, and it can appear once, more than once, or not at all in each of the two levels of narrative. This yields eighteen possible positions. For our purposes, we just need to establish whether the narrative form is singulative (i.e., telling once what happened once—the most common form), repetitive (telling a story event *n* number of times), or iterative (telling once what happened *n* number of times). In "The Last Question," the same question—"How do we reverse entropy?" —is asked of Multivac the computer for the first time in 2061, and thereafter for aeons in a variety of circumstances, but only five instances of this are enacted or dramatized in the narrative.

The first level of organized time—the story level—is, as I have mentioned, something the reader constructs from the discourse level of the text. Some texts, particularly modernist ones, such as the novels of Alain Robbe-Grillet, may deliberately frustrate our desire to determine the chronological order of events. They may not supply enough clues, or they may provide contradictory ones (Alice Walker's *The Color Purple* is somewhat notorious among theorists of narrative for its glaring chronological inconsistencies, which may be authorial mistakes). Asimovian narrative, however, is for the most part very clear and direct in providing clues for the reader. It is usually not too difficult to construct a chronology from the signs he provides in the discourse level of his texts.

Space does not permit me to give a detailed account of how the reader might derive the story of *The End of Eternity* from the discourse level. Instead, having consulted the story summaries written by James Gunn and Joseph Patrouch, I will synopsize the story, elaborating on certain aspects of the plot—particularly those that concern hierarchies of knowledge, which Asimovian narrative nearly always sets up (see the discussion of the Foundation series in chapter 6). This analysis will prepare the way for a discussion of anachronies and their role in *The End of Eternity.*

One of the most paradoxical story elements is the fact that Eternity has its origin in chronological time. The Temporal Field had been invented in the 24th century by a scientist named Vikkor Mallansohn, but it was not until the 27th century that Eternity had been established as a political organization. Apparently the denizens of the 24th century had not had the slightest inkling of what Mallansohn's invention signified. At first Eternity had been set up to handle trade between centuries and, through such trade, to smooth out inequalities among centuries. But gradually—and unbeknownst to humanity—the Eternals had learned proficiency in the techniques of Reality change, altering events so that "the greatest good for the greatest number" would come about.

The Eternals are recruited from various centuries in time at a young age. They live out most of their normal life spans (called physioyears) in Eternity. In other words, they are not eternal, as people in some centuries suppose them to be. They are almost always men, since they, unlike women, can be abstracted from time without the danger of experiencing significant Reality Change. The boys are trained into a kind of caste system that includes Observers, who gather data about the various times; Sociologists, who calculate the effects of change on society; Life-Plotters, who calculate the effects of change on individuals; Computers, who analyze individual acts that will produce desired changes; and Technicians, who effect changes in Reality. (The Observers' ideal of the unemotional, carefully controlled, and meticulously measured accumulation of data most nearly approximates our present-day beliefs about what constitutes normal science.[6]) All Eternals are supposed to strive for the betterment of Reality.

The people of the various centuries know that the Eternals supervise intertemporal trade, which they consider to be their chief function. They also have a dim knowledge that the Eternals somehow prevent disaster from striking mankind. The Eternals therefore constitute a mass father image for the generations and create a certain feeling of security. But humanity is not meant to know that their Reality is being manipulated. The domain of Eternity had gradually extended itself "upwhen" from the 27th century. It had gotten the power to do this by tapping into the nova that our sun eventually becomes. But from 70,000 to 150,000 upwhen (the Hidden Centuries), the Eternals—for reasons they can only speculate about (perhaps a race of supermen is blocking them)—cannot enter time. After the year 150,000 Earth still has living creatures, but mankind has vanished.

The society of the Eternals strikes Andrew Harlan, our viewpoint character and an Eternal himself, as being like a monastic organization of Primitive times (the centuries before Eternity was established, which are unchangeable). Harlan was recruited as a fifteen-year-old from the 95th century. Initially, he was trained for ten years as a Cub, and in his fifth year as an Observer he was assigned to the 482nd century under Computer Hobbe Finge, whom he soon learns to dislike. However, within three months his reports as an Observer are good enough to earn him a post as the Personal Technican to Senior Computer Laban Twissell, one of the most respected men in all Eternity, located in the 575th century. One of his first assignments for Twissell, however, is not to change Reality but to educate a newly inducted Eternal, Brinsley Sheridan Cooper, about Primitive history, which is Harlan's special interest. Cooper is from the 78th century. Although he is ten physioyears younger than Harlan, in another way he is centuries older, since he was born seventeen centuries before him.

After two physioyears, Harlan is reassigned to Finge in the 482nd century on a temporary basis. It seems that Finge needs a very accurate Observation to be done on the 482nd because certain undesirable beliefs about the Eternals have arisen among the ruling classes of this century. Harlan is to be sent to the estate of Noÿs Lambent, a beautiful aristocratic woman who may have already formed a liaison with Finge: the sexual mores of the era are rather liberal, and she has been functioning as Finge's personal secretary in Eternity. When she attempts to seduce Harlan, he quickly finds out that she believes that by making love to an Eternal she too can become eternal. Although he initially dislikes her, Harlan falls in love with Noÿs. Noÿs gives him an intoxicating drug and they make love. In the aftermath of their lovemaking, Harlan experiences strange thoughts, "coming to him at a moment between sense and nonsense," about Mallansohn and Cooper. He becomes convinced that he knows a terrible secret he was not meant to know. Although we are not told what the secret is, we might guess than Mallansohn *is* Cooper, provided that we are familiar enough with the conventions of the time-travel story. Because of the increasing irrationality of his behavior—unusual in an Asimovian hero—we might also suspect that Harlan has been put under some kind of hypnotic suggestion by Noÿs.

On his return to Eternity after several days with Noÿs, Harlan is mocked by Finge with the knowledge that in the new Reality Change, Noÿs will not want him. She may be married or even deformed, Finge suggests. Harlan also finds out that he was manipulated by Finge into his amorous encounter with Noÿs so that Finge could confirm his suspicions about the presence of undesirable attitudes among Timers of the social class to which Noÿs belongs. The whole purpose of Finge's proposed change is to wipe out the superstition about the effects of intimacy with Eternals. Without that superstition, Finge claims, a woman like Noÿs could not possibly want a man like Harlan, who is not at all handsome.

Harlan manages to persuade himself that it does not matter why Noÿs loves him. He vows to have Noÿs before any Reality Change occurs, and he is willing to commit crimes against Eternity to have her, or even to destroy it. In the next month of physiotime Harlan commits a number of crimes. He first pulls Noÿs out of time and races upwhen with her to the untenanted 111,394th century, where he secretes her. During the next few physioweeks he visits her as often as he can, while he moves back to his permanent station at the 575th century and teaches Cooper more Primitive history. On several occasions he goes back to the 482nd to fetch items from Noÿs's house. On the last trip he miscalculates, perhaps because of the thought of the impending Change, and meets himself—a paradoxical event that casts a lingering shadow of horror upon him.

He then searches the summaries of projected Reality Changes as they pass through the Allwhen Council and finds a proposed Reality Change that has been inexpertly computed (a mistake that could result in demotion). Twissell visits Harlan to tell him that the 482nd century has been changed so that the ruling classes of that century, who have the most contact with the Eternals, no longer suspect that the Eternals do much more than supervise intertemporal trade (their main function is to change and regulate Reality). He asks Harlan to meet him the next day in the Computing Room; he has something important to say. With the knowledge of a computing error—minute, but significant in terms of human life—Harlan travels upwhen to the 2456th century and persuades Sociologist Kantor Voy (by threatening to blackmail him) and a Life-Plotter, Neron Feruque, to find out about the nature of Noÿs's analogue in the new Reality. They agree to do so, but only if Harlan himself will effect the Minimum Necessary Change. Voy tells him that the Life-Plotting will take about three hours. During this time, Harlan makes the Change, which has the effect of destroying space travel in the 2481st century. After about three hours of work (on the discourse level, half of the novel is narrated as an analepsis during this interval) they find the answer, to Harlan's delight: Noÿs has no analogue in the new Reality. She could take her position in the new society in the most inconspicuous and convenient manner possible, or she could stay in Eternity. Feruque says he does not quite see how she had fit into the old society. This puzzling notion is a foreshadowing of the revelation that Noÿs is not from the 482nd century.

Harlan rushes back upwhen to tell Noÿs the good news, but finds himself inexplicably blocked at the 100,000th century. The existence of the barrier sends Harlan racing back downwhen to assault Finge with a neuronic whip (a weapon bred out of Reality but kept in Eternity), thinking that Finge has somehow arranged the block across the time shafts. Finge, who denies having done so, tells Harlan that he has observed him all along and reported his activities to the Allwhen Council. Frustrated, Harlan returns to the 575th century and appears before a subcommittee of the Allwhen Council with Twissell. The Council does not interrogate Harlan about Noÿs; instead, Senior Computer Sennor, who represents "normal" science, lectures him on the paradoxes of time travel. Prominent among these paradoxes in the idea of a man meeting himself in time. Sennor analyzes the four structural possibilities of knowledge in such a situation (A knows B, B knows A, both, or neither). Sennor's theory is that Reality, although basically inertial, will always change to avoid paradoxes. In general (and like the psychohistorians of the Foundation series), the Eternals want to breed out of Reality any knowledge of their activities. The insecurities such knowledge would arouse could destroy their plans for humanity (see chapter 6).

After the meeting, Harlan explains to Twissell that he has been studying the mathematics involved in creating the Temporal Field and has discovered that the basic equations did not exist until the research of Jan Verdeer in the 27th century. In effect, he states the precise nature of the time loop to Twissell: "Eternity could never have been established without Mallansohn's discovery of the Temporal field. Mallansohn could never have accomplished this without a knowledge of mathematics that existed only in his future." Thus, he had been helped by someone in the future—most likely Cooper, who had been selected as an Eternal against the rules (he was overaged—twenty-four years old—and married). Twissell admits that the situation has indeed come full circle, but more than Harlan knows: Cooper *is* Mallansohn.

Twissell gives Harlan a biography of Vikkor Mallansohn and tells him of the memoir he had bequeathed to the Eternals by enclosing it in a Time-stasis that could only be opened by the Computers of Eternity. It had remained untouched for three centuries until Henry Wadsman, the first of the great Eternals, had opened it in the 27th century. The memoir had revealed that Mallansohn, or rather Cooper, had been born in the 78th century, had spent some time in Eternity, and had died in the 24th century. The real Mallansohn, a reclusive, eccentric scientist, had died before the Temporal Field had been constructed. Cooper, having previously been sent by Eternity, had taken over Mallansohn's work and identity and created the Field. Anxious that the process of establishing Eternity be somehow quickened, improved, and made more secure, Cooper had written the memoir, which

Twissell now owns and is determined to follow to the letter. That includes keeping Cooper from knowing anything he had not proved he had learned by reference to it in the memoir.

Twissell makes it clear that the intention of the circle in time is to establish the knowledge of how to build Eternity ahead of its natural time. Left to themselves, humans would not have learned the truth about time and the nature of Reality before their technological advances had made racial suicide inevitable. Twissell knows, however, that Harlan can at any moment destroy Eternity by giving Cooper significant information concerning the memoir. Harlan does believe Twissell when Twissell assures him that Noÿs is safe (though we learn later that Twissell does not know about the block in time). Twissell takes Harlan to a room in which a time-travel machine stands. While Harlan is inspecting the control room, Twissell locks him in, because Cooper's memoirs mention that Harlan had been at the controls. Harlan is angered, and his mind is flooded with thoughts of a "Samson-smash of the temple." He appears to pull the switch but, unbeknowst to Twissell, he melts the locking mechanism with the neuronic whip and frees the thrust control that directs the time-travel machine, sending Cooper downwhen. Harlan tells Twissell what he has done and waits for Eternity to vanish.

When this does not immediately happen, Twissell trys to explain that there are an infinite number of cycles in the Mallansohn Reality. Because Harlan had met himself, Twissell speculates, Reality had had to change to prevent the meeting. In the changed Reality, Harlan had not sent Cooper back to the 24th century. Twissell thinks they might still be able to destroy the threat to Eternity by trying to undo what Harlan has done. To win Harlan's sympathy in the endeavor, Twissell reveals to Harlan that he too had committed a crime of desire in the past. He had loved a woman, a Timer from the 575th century. When she had become pregnant, he had refused to have the pregnancy terminated (no Eternal may have a child). He had lived to see his son become an aeronautic engineer. But when a Reality Change had been proposed in which his son was no longer alive, he obeyed his oath as an Eternal and allowed the Change to transpire. Unfortunately, the worst possible thing happened: an analogue of his son did exist in the new reality—a paraplegic from the age of four. Hence, one of the announced themes of the book is that women are the flaw in Eternity.

This story of a desire for human rootedness in time moves Harlan enough to agree to search in his Primitive history materials for a message across time from Cooper. Three days later Harlan finally discovers the message, woven into a magazine advertisement. When read anachronistically and anagramatically, it reveals that Cooper is stranded in 1932. The key iconic sign is a drawing of an atomic mushroom cloud. It catches Harlan's eye immediately. Cooper had known it would out of "sheer anachronism."[7] At the same time, it has no meaning for anyone in 1932. Harlan wants to withhold this information from Twissell until Noÿs is safe with him. He and Twissell journey upwhen to try to reach her. During the trip, Twissell explains some of the history of Eternity and speculates about the reasons for the barrier. With all their manipulations of Reality, the Eternals had changed the human environment to the extent that mankind had basically stopped evolving. Perhaps, Twissell suggests, the Eternals had done this on purpose because they did not want to meet a race of supermen from the future. Although most Changes extend only through a few centuries before temporal inertia causes their effects to die out, perhaps this race of supermen had found out somehow that their reality was being subtly tampered with, and it was they who had set up the barrier.

Harlan experiences a momentary terror when he thinks that the supermen may possess Noÿs. But when he and Twissell arrive at the 100,000th century there is no barrier, and Noÿs is waiting for them. The absence of a barrier is disturbing to Harlan. He insists that Noÿs accompany him in the time-travel machine back to 1932 in his attempt to rescue Cooper. They discover traces of Cooper in a cave outside of Denver, Colorado, but before they search for him, Harlan confront Noÿs with his suspicion that she may be one of the supermen, manipulating Finge and him alike for her own purposes. When Harlan threatens to kill her, she admits to being from the 111,394th century, but not to being of a race of supermen. The people of the Hidden Centuries are *Homo sapiens*—ordinary people. The scientists of her time, who do possess time travel (although it is based on different postulates than those of the Eternals), had looked into mankind's future 50,000 years. Sometime after the 125,000th century, mankind had solved the secret of the interstellar drive—had learned how to manage the Jump through interstellar space. Finally, humans could reach the stars. Mankind had tried to leave Earth, but found the Galaxy already inhabited by alien intelligences. Mankind drew back its exploratory feelers and remained at home, knowing the Earth for what it was: a prison surrounded by an infinity of freedom. And then, robbed of its challenges, mankind died out.

The people of Noÿs's time had learned indirectly of the existence of Eternity in the past. They had discovered that they were living in a Reality of very low probability with regard to another Reality, the Basic State, which encompassed all of their analogues and had the maximum probability. This meant that some Change initiated by Eternity in the far downwhen had managed, through the workings of statistical chance, to alter the Basic State all the way up to their century and beyond. The people of Noÿs's time had seen this alteration as an evil because the Basic State had contained many happinesses, many goods, infinite variety.

A hierarchy of knowledge begins to emerge in the book, as it does in all Asimov's narrative worlds: The Eternals smile at the ignorance of the Timers, who know only one Reality, but Noÿs's supermen smile at the ignorance of the Eternals, who think that there are many Realities but that only one exists at a time. The people of Noÿs's time had been able to perceive alternate realities, not calculate them. They see them in their state of non-Reality.

Harlan and Noÿs set out to undo the evil that Eternity had done. After setting up the quarantined area of the Hidden Centuries and investigating their past and future time line, they had come up with a plan to send Noÿs into the past to destroy Eternity. However, Harlan is now bent on preserving Eternity because he feels that he has been betrayed by his love for Noÿs—that he is nothing more than a marionette whose strings are pulled by everyone else. Noÿs tries to assure Harlan that she loves him. Before accepting her assignment, she had studied the Realities at her disposal. She had chosen the one in which Harlan had misdirected Cooper—in which she and he, together, had returned to the Primitive, living in it for the rest of their days, happily loving each other. Noÿs intends to alter Primitive history by sending a letter to "a man of Italy" who will begin experimenting with the neutronic bombardment of uranium (this can only be Enrico Fermi, who won the Nobel Prize in 1938 for his research in physics, which eventually led to the invention of the atomic bomb).

In this time line, there is a probability that the Earth will end, with a largely radioactive crust. This may not be an entirely bad development if it drives mankind into space. Noÿs points out the negative aspects of Eternity, which have become more and more obvious to Harlan. If Eternity had never been established, for instance, the energies that had gone into temporal engineering would have gone into nucleonics instead. Eternity would not have come, but the interstellar drive would have, and much earlier. The mere fact of Eternity's existence has wiped out the Galactic Empire, and with it mankind's strivings. Under the force of Noÿs's arguments, Harlan begins to see Eternity "with great clarity as a sink of deepening psychoses, a writhing pit of abnormal motivation, a mass of desperate lives torn brutally out of context."[8] He chooses not to find Cooper, and the time-travel machine disappears, signaling the end of Eternity and the beginning of Infinity.

The preceding story summary has been arranged, insofar as possible, in conformity with chronological order—which of course eliminates the surprises that Asimov so carefully staged for the reader's delight. But as I mentioned at the beginning of this chapter, to study the temporal order of a narrative is to study both the events and how we learn about those events. Furthermore, it is "to compare the order in which events or temporal sections are arranged in the narrative discourse with the order of succession these same events or temporal segments have in the story."[9] In the remaining space of this chapter, I cannot offer the kind of microanalysis that Gerard Genette offers for Proust. Nonetheless, I do want to annotate the main features of the temporal articulation of the discourse level of *The End of Eternity,* which are superimposed over the story level and rearrange it into a field of anachronies, composed of both retrospection (analepsis) and anticipation (prolepsis). To make my observations more concise, I will discuss the articulation of temporal order in this text and briefly touch on duration and frequency.

The actual amount of time elapsed in *The End of Eternity* cannot be more than a week, and may be considerably less. We can detect or infer the duration of the period elapsed through statements or clues at the discourse level. At the outset of the novel we find Harlan racing upwhen to blackmail Kantor Voy into doing a Life-Plot for Noÿs. This opening scene, in medias res, is properly the now of the story and the beginning of the first narrative's temporal field. For a brief moment story and discourse coincide, as they do in the blackmail scenes, which represent about three hours (they are mainly in chapters 1 and 6). We do not return to the steadily progressing now of the story until chapter 10, in which Harlan reaches the time barrier at the 100,000th century. The intervening narrative consists mainly of analepses whose reach, extent, and content will be commented on below.

Following close upon Harlan's journey upwhen to the barrier is his angry return to Finge. The next day he appears before the Allwhen Council. A few hours later he contrives to maroon Cooper in the Primitive time but agrees to save him after hearing Twissell's story. The search for the advertisement takes three days and is related mostly in summary, but the analysis of the actual message is presented as a dramatic scene. We are not told exactly how much time elapses before the day of departure of the "rescue" mission, but Twissell has to consult the Allwhen Council about the mission's feasibility—an event that is almost entirely elided on the discourse level. However, the time spent in the Primitive era by Harlan and Noÿs—presented mostly in dramatic scenes—extends from late afternoon of the day of their arrival there to the dawn of the following day.

Thus, we may take the extent of the first narrative's temporal field to be about a week. Any section of the discourse that refers or alludes to events outside this time frame is an anachrony—either reaching into the past to supply needed information about the background of the characters or of the history of the institution of Eternity, or reaching forward to convey information about the future (necessarily always partial, since this kind of information tends to destroy suspense). The analepses are primarily homodiegetic—that is, concerned with the main story of Andrew Harlan. Others are heterodiegetic, such as the story Twissell tells of his past in chapter 14. The reach of the homodiegetic analepses can extend as far back as Harlan's early memories of his mother, or his later education as an Eternal. The former does not extend very far into the first narrative, and in fact breaks off in an ellipsis. The latter extends through all of Harlan's education as an Eternal (seventeen years) and links up seamlessly with the first narrative, although it interrupts it (mainly chapters 2, 3, and 4). Most of the analepses are concerned with the events of the preceding month, in which Harlan had met and fallen in love with Noÿs and committed his crimes against Eternity (chapters 7, 8, and 9). These are presented mostly in dramatic scenes, with some interlinking summaries.

The prolepses of the book (apart from the minor foreshadowings mentioned earlier in the story summary) are mainly concentrated in the later chapters—especially the last, chapter 18, in which Noÿs tells Harlan the story of the supermen. It is here that we learn what happened in the Hidden Centuries (Harlan's future, their past) and how humans investigated their future and discovered the Basic State. Of course, the Mallansohn memoir is also Harlan's future, but a more immediate one, more closely linked with the actual moment of narration and therefore more internal to the time field of the first narrative. One prolepsis that is dramatized effectively can be found in chapter 6, in which Harlan effects a Reality Change in the 2456th century, the results of which can be viewed in the 2481st. Almost instantaneously, as Harlan applies "the Touch" in the 2456th century, a spaceport is blasted in the 2481th, and its once-shiny buildings become rusted and reduced in stature. Harlan's Touch wipes out space travel. Because the reader is asked to imagine viewing both centuries simultaneously on screens, this chapter represents another attempt at paradoxical anachrony. It asks us to imagine successive events simultaneously (or nearly so; we must not forget the text's linearity).

This type of analysis reveals some of the complex layering of time in the book. And how else to speculate on a possible science of time travel? As a scientist, Asimov does not admit to the possibility of time travel; the idea simply violates too many known laws of nature. But he is willing, in the context of a fictional construct, to investigate the structural permutations of the idea. He says that he designed the book in such a way as to make it "the ultimate example of the type" and that he tried to bring into play every time-travel paradox he could, matching the construction of the book with the complexity of the concept.[10]

It must be pointed out that competent readers have had difficulties with the book on a first reading. Damon Knight, a noted science-fiction author himself, complained about the extremely complex background of the society of Eternals, which the reader does not have a fair chance to absorb before he is flung into the story proper. Once he passed this initial barrier, however, Knight found the book structured according to an "incisive logic" in which plot and counterplot wind up spectacularly together in an acceptable happy ending.[11] Other critics have complained not about the background but about the narrative structure. Joseph Patrouch, for instance, points out the nonchronologies of the story level, in which almost all of the main characters are involved (e.g., Mallansohn, or Cooper, is born in the 78th century, spends some time in Eternity—in the 575th century—and dies in the 24th). In Patrouch's view, to narrate the novel nonchronologically is to complicate the discourse level with "mere obfuscation"[12] (I have substituted narratologic terms for Patrouch's). Perhaps Patrouch is missing what another critic, James Gunn, has pointed out about the book: it is concerned with the rational exploration of the varieties of time, with the idea that mankind must learn to live with uncertainty; therefore, its narrative complexity is a mirror of its thematic concerns.[13]

When it comes to the certainty of scientific truth, *The End of Eternity* is indeed one of Asimov's least authoritarian works. Asimov's views on the nature of scientific truth (as opposed to philosophical truth) have much in common with those of Karl Popper, though they should perhaps not be identified with them entirely. Popper is famous for arguing that science does not give us sure and certain knowledge, a foundation on which to make true statements about the world. For Popper the criterion of the scientific status of a theory is its falsifiability, refutability, or testability. The method of science, then, is criticism (i.e., attempted falsification); Popper called his philosophy of science "critical rationalism."[14] Similarly, Asimov remarks that "The uniqueness of science comes in this: the scientific method offers a way of determining the False. Science is the only gateway to proven error."[15]

To put it concisely, *The End of Eternity* is a book that dramatizes the collision of "normal" science with the notion of critical rationalism. For in constructing this anachronistic narrative of the attempted foundation of a science of time travel, Asimov does not confirm the Eternal Sennor's verities about the conservative nature of Reality. Nor does he allow Twissell to verify the authority of the Mallansohn memoir, which operates like a paradigm. On the contrary, what he affirms is change—radical innovation—which can only come about when a theory is exposed to the risk of refutation. It is because the supermen, who supposedly possess a theory of time travel based on different postulates, expose that theory to possible refutation that such change happens. In short, we have a science-fiction novel in which the reader sees the idea of "normal" science as an established practice in which accepted theories are confirmed or adjusted, tested by a critical rationalism that develops through an often unsettling interplay of temporal paradoxes.

# *Chapter Three*
# The Robot Stories

## Asimov's Noble Robots

Asimov's robot stories are collected in five volumes: *I, Robot* (1950), *The Rest of the Robots* (1964), *The Complete Robot* (1982), *Robot Dreams* (1986), and *Robot Visions* (1990). The last two volumes contain only a few previously uncollected robot stories, and the third volume is an omnibus in which previously published stories are arranged topically. *I, Robot* is by most critical accounts one of the most influential books in the history of modern science fiction because it established new conventions for writing robot stories. For instance, in Asimov's stories, robots were presented as human artifacts rationally engineered for human happiness. By their very nature, Asimov's robots could not turn menacingly against their human masters and destroy them in the manner of Frankenstein's monster. But more important, and largely because of the Three Laws of Robotics, Asimov's robots seemed noble and decent—often more so than their human counterparts. Thus, Asimov did much in his stories to counter the Faustian image of science that had arisen in the public imagination. Prejudice against machines and technology is in fact the constant background, if not the subject matter, of the robot stories. Two refer explicitly to the operation of a "Frankenstein complex" about robots ("Little Lost Robot" in *I, Robot* and "Lenny" in *The Rest of the Robots*).

Asimov's robot stories also have predicted certain real developments. Robotics is now recognized as a field of study, and computer-controlled machines are now in industrial use. In addition, Asimov added two new words to the English language through these stories. The *Oxford English Dictionary* credits him with the earliest uses of *robotics* and *positronic*. He coined both words while in his twenties.[1]

Most of the discussion in this chapter will focus on the first two volumes of robot stories—primarily on *I, Robot,* in which the Three Laws of Robotics were first articulated. I will be concerned mainly with characterizing the science of these stories, not with analyzing their literary aspects (aside from narrative structure). While characterization is often considered of prime importance in mainstream literary efforts, such has not been the case for science fiction for most of its history. Asimov has never been too concerned with developing convincing characters.[2] Even Susan Calvin, chief robopsychologist for United States Robots—a character who analyzes and interprets robot behavior (she appears in about a dozen stories), and a character touted by Asimov as one of his most well-rounded—is little more than a stereotype (the frigid woman scientist who gives up family for career). Asimov has openly acknowledged his lack of interest in literary matters and has defended his mode of writing. He has declared that he is not interested in style, characterization, or poetic metaphor, but in ideas. Asimov considers science fiction a branch of literature that exists for the purpose of presenting scientific ideas. He takes credit for three ideas of importance to the world of science fiction, each of which he has exploited to the full: the all-human Galaxy, psychohistory, and (most important) the Three Laws of Robotics.

The analysis in this chapter will focus on the Three Laws of Robotics and how they functioned as a kind of scientific paradigm that guided the writing of a whole body of fiction. The all-human Galaxy and pyschohistory (an extraordinary science, or one "in crisis," in Thomas Kuhn's terms) will be discussed in chapter 5. At this point the reader may want to review note 6 of chapter 2, which situates Asimov in the tradition of normal science, before reading further in this chapter.

## Robotics as "Normal" Science

The Three Laws of Robotics are stated at the outset of *I, Robot:* "1.) A robot may not injure a human being, or, through inaction, allow a human being to come to harm, 2.) A robot must obey the orders given it by human beings except where such orders would conflict with the First Law, and 3.) A robot must protect its own existence as long as such protection does not conflict with the First or Second Law" (p. 6). These laws are supposedly quoted from a textbook, the *Handbook of Robotics* (56th edition, 2058 A.D.). As Kuhn indicates, one of the surest signs of the presence of normal science is the appearance of its pedagogic form in textbooks, which expound the body of accepted theory, illustrate many or all of its successful applications, and compare these applications with exemplary observations and experiments. In normal science, both scientists and laypeople take much of their image of creative scientific activity from these authoritative textual sources rather than from actual experimentation on nature. These texts are the means by which we learn "the vocabulary and syntax of a contemporary scientific language" and acquire the rules of the game.[3]

By quoting his Laws of Robotics (in Asimov, the term *robot* includes computers) at the outset of his story, Asimov gives us the impression that we are already operating within the confines of a new science. Indeed, in the framing story that organizes the other stories into a short-story cycle, the newspaper reporter interviewing Susan Calvin cannot remember a world without robots. The Laws thus function, in a fictional context, as a verbal representation of the paradigm of a "new" science, robotics. They are not, of course, strict scientific definitions. Asimov assumes their meaning to be specified by cybernetics, a mathematical psychology of thinking machines, and by the fictional technological marvel that is the positronic brain—"a spongy globe of platinum-iridium" about the size of a human brain, but one in which "brain paths" are "marked out" (and are therefore open to scientific observation and manipulation) by the production and destruction of positrons. Positrons were discovered in cosmic rays in 1932, but their existence had been theorized earlier. By incorporating them in his robot stories, Asimov includes actual science in the stories' shared background.

Asimov does not systematically present the scientific concepts underlying the new science. Instead, he works out the inherent verbal and situational ambiguities in the Three Laws, which provide him with the conflicts and uncertainties required for new stories. To Asimov's great relief, "it always seemed possible to think up a new angle out of the sixty-one words of the Three Laws."[4] As Kuhn has demonstrated, the paradigm that provides the basis for a new tradition of scientific research never completely resolves all of its problems. In fact, resolving these puzzles and problems becomes the primary activity of scientists working within the paradigm. For Kuhn, as for Asimov, paradigms are constitutive elements of science, and the object of normal science is to solve a puzzle or problem whose very existence is assumed to confirm the validity of the paradigm. Normal science is, then, an enterprise that aims to refine, extend, and articulate a paradigm already in existence. According to Kuhn, one of the most important foci for research in normal science is empirical work (which may include the "instrumentation" of a theory in the field testing of scientific equipment) undertaken "to articulate the paradigm theory, resolving some of its residual ambiguities and permitting the solution of problems to which it had previously only drawn attention."[5]

Hence, that most of Asimov's robot stories take the narrative form of a puzzle or problem is no accident. With these stories, Asimov is trying to represent a period of normal science in which robotics has already been established. He seeks to convey to the reader the intellectual pleasures of using ingenuity in the puzzle solving that occurs within a new scientific paradigm.

*I, Robot* opens in the year 2057, when Susan Calvin is seventy-five years old and retiring from U.S. Robots. The reporter interviewing her has collected all of the basic biographical data about her, but presses her for a "human-interest angle" to enliven his account. She responds by telling him the story of Robbie, a nursemaid robot. Robbie was constructed in 1996 as a nonspeaking robot and sold to the Weston family as a nursemaid for their daughter, Gloria. Soon Gloria develops such an affection for Robbie, who is engineered to be a perfect playmate, that she will not play with other children. Her mother in turn develops an unreasoning hatred of robots and expresses the main prejudices against them (e.g., they are soulless, they cannot be trusted with human children). Although her husband explains to her that the robot is incapable of harming Gloria because of the First Law, the mother wins out, and Robbie is sent back to U.S. Robots.

Gloria is devastated by the loss. Eventually, her parents decide to attack the problem psychologically, by attempting to convince Gloria that Robbie is a machine and not a person. They arrange a visit to U.S. Robots. While touring the factory, Gloria inadvertantly exposes herself to danger, and Robbie saves her life. Having witnessed her daughter's rescue at the robot's hands, Mrs. Weston grudgingly agrees to let Robbie return to live with the family "until he rusts."

"Robbie" is the only story in *I, Robot* that shows a robot used in a family context ("Satisfaction Guaranteed," in *The Rest of the Robots,* is another). As such, it functions as a human interest story that involves us emotionally. Perhaps this story is placed where it is to counter assertions that Asimov is too cerebral a writer. Ironically, it also goes a long way toward demonstrating what Susan Calvin believes about robots: they are a "cleaner, better breed" than we are.

In the other stories of *I, Robot,* Asimov concerns himself with more cognitive issues. By the year 2002 U.S. Robots had invented the mobile speaking robot, which had aroused more prejudice. Soon most world governments banned robot use on Earth for anything other than scientific research between 2002 and 2007. U.S. Robots was forced to exploit the extraterrestrial market. The three stories that follow "Robbie" are about the field testing of robots on Mercury, at a space station, and in the asteroids. Checking the workings of the experimental robots are a pair of wisecracking engineers named Powell and Donovan. Their solving of puzzles and problems presented by the basic design of the robot brain represents the endeavors of normal science.

"Runaround" is about a new type of robot, SPD-13 (Speedy), designed to work in the mines of Mercury. As the story opens, the robot has been sent out to retrieve some selenium for the team's photocell banks, which will soon fail without it, allowing the full force of the sun to enter the mining station. However, Speedy has not returned. Powell and Donovan search for the robot and eventually find it circling a pool of selenium, seemingly drunk (it sings snatches from Gilbert and Sullivan). Through a combination of observation and deduction based on the Three Laws of Robotics, the team arrives at the truth: Speedy is stuck in an equilibrium between the potentials of laws 2 and 3. That is, Speedy had responded to an order by human beings to retrieve the selenium (Law 2) but had found, and had sought to avoid, a danger to himself at the site (Law 3). The team infers the presence of a volatile iron carbonyl, given off by volcanic action, that threatens to corrode Speedy's positronic circuits. The solution is finally found when Powell decides to get outside of both laws by appealing to the transcendent First Law of Robotics. By exposing himself to the sun, he puts himself in a life-threatening situation, and Speedy snaps out of his confusion to rescue him.

In addition to being one of Asimov's most cognition-oriented robot stories, "Runaround" is a classic story of normal science, for the paradigm makes possible both the problem and its expected solution. The paradigm itself is never questioned or put at serious risk. Although Powell risks his life, he does so with every confidence that Speedy will behave in accordance with the Three Laws (unless Speedy's circuits are too damaged for him to respond). Incidentally, the word *robotics* first appeared in print in this story, and the Three Laws of Robotics were first explicitly formulated (*Astounding,* March 1942).

"Reason," the next story, takes place on a space power station that beams power from the sun to Earth and the other inhabited planets. U.S. Robots has developed a new kind of robot, QT-1 (Cutie), to direct the energy beams. Upon completion of their Mercury assignment, Donovan and Powell are sent to the station to field-test the robot. This time the problem is of a more speculative nature. It seems that Cutie is caught up in a paradigm that is completely different from the one in which Donovan and Powell operate. Because he is superior in intelligence and strength to the pair, he deduces that he could have been created only by a being more powerful than they: the energy converter, which he reasons must be a god.

No matter what Powell and Donovan do—they even construct a robot in his presence—Cutie cannot see them as more powerful. He is a complete Cartesian, deducing "the absolute Truth" from the "clear light of rigid reason." Evidently, he is also a parody of the rational robot. Cutie appears to break the Second Law of Robotics by disobeying Donovan and Powell. But when Cutie handles the energy beam perfectly during an electron storm, the two engineers decide that he has not really violated the Laws of Robotics. They reason that the laws account for Cutie's refusal to obey them: "Obedience is the Second Law. No harm to humans is the first. How can he keep humans from harm, whether he knows it or not? Why, by keeping the energy beam stable. He *knows* he can keep it more stable than we can, since he insists he's the superior being, so he *must* keep us out of the control room. It's inevitable if you consider the Laws of Robotics."[6]

The reasoning here may seem a bit specious, especially in view of the self-consciousness Asimov attributes to Cutie ("whether he knows it or not"), but the team decides to leave Cutie to function with his religious delusion, since it apparently works so well. Notwithstanding its philosophic concern with religion, the story clearly demonstrates a flaw in the nature of reason itself: there is no reason for us to be reasonable. Postulates are based on assumptions and adhered to by faith. Furthermore, once we are within a system of "self-evident" postulates—or a paradigm—we do not normally question it. Cutie literally does not see the same objects as do Donovan and Powell. He believes that the stars outside the station are an optical illusion. As Kuhn has observed, the competition between paradigms (which, among other things, define the nature and kinds of objects in the universe) is not the sort of battle that can be resolved by proofs. Paradigms are incommensurable. Because they are within different paradigms, the two engineers and the Cartesian robot are bound partly to talk past each other.[7] In the last analysis, however, Cutie's behavior does not violate any of the Three Laws, and so the paradigm is not invalidated by any counterinstances.

In "Catch That Rabbit," which takes place the following year (2016), Powell and Donovan are sent to the asteroids to deal with a multiple mining robot—a "master robot," DV-5 (Dave), which has six subrobots, or "fingers," working under it. This story deals not with religious mania but with a seeming amnesia and violation of the Second Law. Dave and his subrobots have not been producing any ore and cannot remember why this is so. The two engineers, after consulting the Handbook of Robotics, are not sure what kind of robot error is involved. They decide to observe Dave's behavior in an emergency, when his personal initiative would be expected to be most strained. They create a mild cave-in and deduce what type of order Dave has been sending to the other robots via his positronic field. They discover that Dave needs to have his personal initiative circuit expanded so that he can work without humans present.

As in the previous two stories, the narrative proceeds according to the narrative schema of normal science. First a problem is discovered, "facts" are gathered with the guidance of the paradigm, some theorizing takes place, and a clever solution is found. Although they joke about it, the two engineers are proud of the part they play in the development of new robots and in "aiding scientific advance." As Kuhn indicates, the unit of normal scientific achievement is the solved problem, and these two characters, to our amusement and intellectual delight, have become masters of that game.[8]

The next story, "Liar," takes place on Earth in the year 2021, when Susan Calvin is thirty-eight. It is one of Asimov's best robot stories, for it plays out in a kind of permutational game all of the cognitive positions of narrative knowledge: truth (being + appearing), falsehood (not being + not appearing), secret (being + not appearing), and delusion or lie (not being + appearing). With this elementary semiotic square, it is possible to gauge the truthfulness of the characters and determine whether events will be true, false, secretive, or delusive.[9]

The robot of this story is RB-34 (Herbie), who through a fluke of the manufacturing process can read minds. Naturally, the top officers of U.S. Robots want to keep Herbie's powers a secret, even from other members of the company, until they can announce that they have complete control of the phenomenon. As chief robopsychologist, Susan Calvin is called in on the case. She soon finds that Herbie is not interested in human science, which he calls "just a mass of collected data plastered together by makeshift theory." He is interested in fiction, because it tells him about human minds, which he finds incredibly complicated.

What we next figure out, but what the characters are unaware of, is that because of the requirements of the First Law, Herbie tells people the things they most want to hear. Thus he tells Susan Calvin that Milton Ashe, the youngest officer of U.S. Robots, is in love with her, which is not true. Calvin tries to make herself more attractive to Ashe but succeeds only in confusing him and deluding herself until the painfully embarrassing moment when Ashe announces his engagement. Herbie also tells two other scientists that their mutually contradictory mathematics are correct, and gives them false information about who will be the next director of the company. All of the characters act on the information Herbie gives them, not questioning it because it is what they want to hear. Of course, Susan Calvin becomes furious with Herbie. Even though the robot pleads that he could not help being false, she renders him inoperative by presenting him with an insoluble dilemma: it hurts to be told the truth, but it also hurts not to be told the truth.

The next two stories—both set in the year 2029—are important because they tell the story of the development of a hyperatomic drive for interstellar travel, which the robots (i.e., the computers) help to invent. This drive gives human beings the opportunity to create the Galactic Empire. In "Little Lost Robot," the main research on "the problem of the Drive" is being conducted at Hyperbase, a station situated in the asteroid belt. U.S. Robots has created an experimental group of robots, NS-2 (Nestors), some of which have been impressioned with a weakened version of the First Law so that they can work with humans in situations involving radiation. In other words, although they still cannot harm human beings themselves, they have no compulsion to prevent them from being harmed by an extraneous agency. The robot referred to in the title, one of the Nestors, has been told by a frustrated scientist to "get lost." Since robots understand human orders literally, he disappears, hiding himself among sixty-two other robots identical to himself. The task facing Susan Calvin is to find out which of the sixty-three robots is the lost one. She begins her investigation by reasoning out the psychological consequences of impressioning robots with a weakened First Law and determines that a robot so modified would be unstable and might develop a superiority complex. When she learns that only this type of robot can detect gamma radiation, she devises an ingenious test in which the robot's belief in its superiority to human beings betrays it. The main point of the story is to establish the balanced functioning of the paradigm of robotics and to indicate that problems arise when the First Law is weakened.

The seventh story, "Escape," is set on Earth. It brings together Donovan, Powell, and Calvin in an account of how the Brain, a computer impressed with the personality of a child, finally solves the problem of interstellar travel. It seems that the problem with asking the Brain to develop an interstellar drive lies not in any known limitation of its intellectual capacity but in the Robotic Laws. The Brain cannot supply a solution to a problem set before it if arriving at that solution would involve the death or injury of human beings, and travel through hyperspace is thought to be dangerous. The Brain, however, is eventually able to escape this dilemma (which burned out another computer) because its mind of a child is more resilient and because Calvin depresses the importance of the First Law. The Brain helps build an interstellar spaceship that goes through a space warp, taking Powell and Donovan with it. They "die" temporarily but are restored to life when the ship emerges from the space warp. During their "deaths," the Brain effects a partial escape from reality by developing a sense of humor and playing practical jokes on the two engineers. Just how the Brain manages to keep the two alive remains his "prize little joke."

Eventually the Jump through hyperspace is perfected. By 2032 humanoid robots are possible and may have been constructed. "Evidence" deals with the problem of discerning such a robot from a human being.

Stephen Byerley is a district attorney running for mayor of the city in which U.S. Robots is located. The political opposition thinks that Byerley is in fact a robot and accuses the company of a political plot to put one of their own in power. Byerley insists on his rights as a presumptive human being and will not submit to any tests, such as an x-ray examination. The opposition is thus unable to prove that Byerley is a robot; they can only accept the (apparent) proof that he is not a robot if he invalidates one of the Robotic Laws.

During a political speech at the high point of his campaign, Byerley strikes a heckler in front of media representatives—something a robot could not do. But after the election, Susan Calvin speculates that the "person" struck may have been a robot. It is clear that she believes that Byerley is a robot, not least because of his fundamentally decent behavior.

Gradually, the presence of complex computing machines brings about a Golden Age in which they control the economy for humanity's benefit. The major political entities in the world are no longer nations but Regions. The ideological wars of the past century—whether the world would be capitalist or Marxist—seem no longer inevitable in this time prosperity made possible by the positronic robots. Humankind has lived through its torment to witness "the inevitable wasting away of inevitability."

When the Regions of the Earth had formed their Federation in 2044, Byerley had become the first World Co-ordinator. "The Evitable Conflict" takes place in 2052, when he is completing his second term. Byerley tells Susan Calvin about his investigation into small problems with the economy that should not be occurring. Together they discuss the hypotheses suggested by the situation. Some elements of society are still against the machines, but they rule them out as the culprits because the machines are smart enough to take into account any group's resistance to them. The machines deal with such resistance by creating small failures and blaming them on subversive individuals, who are consequently reassigned to less important positions in the system.

Susan Calvin concludes that there is nothing wrong. The first duty of the machines is to preserve themselves for us, because they are now operating under the Robotic Laws for all of humanity. These cybernetic machines have gained absolute control over the economy. In her view, this will make all human conflicts finally evitable; from now on, she says, only the machines are inevitable. The steady progress of normal science has brought about a situation in which only the machines can know the ultimate purpose of humanity. Although humankind seems to have lost any voice in its own future, the emergence of another, more extraordinary science—psychohistory—will restore some control to humanity.

Of Asimov's later robot stories, the one most closely bound to *I, Robot* is "Risk," which is collected in *The Rest of the Robots.* As Asimov himself points out, the story is a sequel to "Little Lost Robot." It involves a different problem but the same human characters and, especially, "the same research problem."[10] That problem, the reader may remember, was the development of the interstellar drive. The story is set on Hyperbase at a time when the drive has been tested but not yet perfected. The animals that had been sent on the test voyage of the ship *Parsec* have returned mindless.

A robot is instructed to pilot the craft on its next flight, but nothing happens at the appointed time. Dr. Mayer Schloss, who at forty is the "grand old man" of the young science of hyperfield matrices, insists that there is nothing wrong with the basic theory; there must be a mechanical failure somewhere on the ship. Over strenuous objections, Susan Calvin sends a man, Dr. Black (the same scientist who told the robot to get lost in "Little Lost Robot"), to investigate—not a robot. At the risk of his life (the ship may be launched into hyperspace by the slightest vibration), Black must discover the failure and determine a safe way of disconnecting the field. He finds the robot frozen at the controls. Having interpreted literally the order to pull firmly back on the controls, the robot had exerted excessive force and bent the control bar.

On the scientific level, the story affirms that theories have to be exposed to the risk of invalidation, but the practical point of the story seems to be that a robot needs to be given a precise order. Unlike a human being, a robot cannot correct his own mistakes without further orders. "Find out what's wrong" is not an order that can be given to a robot. The science of robotics has not yet developed a robotic brain that can learn.

That step is taken in the following story, "Lenny." This story also involves Susan Calvin, who must use the science of robopyschology to explore the mind of a robot that has the mind of a child as the result of being randomly programmed through an accident. Although other scientists see the robot as "abysmally useless" because it has no job to perform and is hence seemingly outside the paradigm of normal robotics, Calvin sees great potential in it. Her study of the robot's positronic brain paths leads her to realize that this robot could lead to "a completely new field of research" that might result in breakthroughs toward solving the abstract problem of how to teach robots. Of course, one problem with beginning with ignorant robots such as Lenny would be that one could never entirely trust the First Law; nonetheless, a research institute could be set up on the moon.

Calvin points out that precisely because of the danger involved, this new area of robotics is likely to attract young researchers. Now that robots are forbidden on Earth, there is already something unpopular, even staid, about being a roboticist.

Calvin ingeniously assimilates an anomaly into the paradigm of normal robotics, which itself will have to be modified in order to result in scientific progress. The goal: to make robots as versatile as human beings. The new branch of robotics that Calvin envisions is, however, still normal science, which is cumulative and owes its success to the ability of scientists to select problems that can be solved by conceptual and instrumental techniques close to those already in existence. Indeed, Calvin already knows what she is looking for when she asks to conduct more tests on the "pseudo-robot" Lenny.

According to Kuhn, unanticipated novelty, the really new discovery, can emerge only to the extent that the scientist's anticipations about his object and his instruments prove incorrect.[11] So far as I know, this never happens in any of Asimov's robot stories, which is why I have called his robotics a normal science. Furthermore, the stories in *I, Robot* form a kind of history of robotics that follows narrative schemas associated with normal science: science as cumulation and puzzle solving.

In closing, it should point out that such anomalies as we find in these stories are not always so happily integrated into the context of normal science, if at all. As a robopsychologist concerned with maintaining the "normalcy" and decency of robots, Susan Calvin wants no unbalanced robots around to antagonize religious fundamentalists or trade unionists, the two groups opposed to her and her science. Thus, the mind-reading robot in "Liar" is destroyed, and the robot with the superiority complex in "Little Lost Robot" is defeated. In one of Asimov's most recent robot stories, "Robot Dreams" (published in 1986; collected in *Robot Dreams*), Susan Calvin deals with a robot who can dream and who manifests unconscious desires to be a human being and to lead his people out of slavery. This plot recalls the early stories about stereotyped robots who turned against their makers—the sort of stories that had led Asimov to formulate the Three Laws of Robotics. But the robot's dreams reveal Asimov's awareness of the potential of an unconscious layer of thought beneath the obvious positronic brain paths—a layer that is not necessarily under the control of the Three Laws. Quite rightly, Calvin senses the danger of a robotic unconscious. She promptly destroys the robot with an electron gun. This story makes it clear that although Asimov is willing to recognize the effects and products of the unconscious, he is not going to tolerate their decentering or disrupting the rationality of normal science.

# *Chapter Four*
# The Robot Novels

## Murder and Robotics

Asimov's four robot novels are generic hybrids. That is, they combine elements of detective fiction and science fiction. The science-fiction elements of these four connected novels derive mainly from sociological extrapolation—the projection of trends in our present society into the far or near future. I will discuss the "socio-logic" underlying the novels before I examine their narrative structures.

The robot novels depict a society, some three millennia into the future, in which a radical change has taken place in human culture. That change has been the gradual formation of City culture. Almost all human beings now live in massive, self-contained steel-and-concrete Cities, the "caves of steel" of the first novel's title. There are some eight hundred Cities on Earth, with an average population of ten million.

New York City, the setting of *The Caves of Steel* (1954), has spread to encompass over two thousand square miles and has a population of over twenty million. Asimov makes it clear at the outset of the novel that the Cities arose because they were the most rational and organized way of dealing with the population explosion, which still threatens Earth. With their miles of factories, hydroponic plants, and yeast-culture vats, which surround the residential sections connected and interlaced by expressways and moving sidewalk "strips," which in turn surround an enormous central complex of administrative offices, the Cities are certainly "the culmination of man's mastery over the environment." But living in these weather-controlled, womblike environments has taken its toll on human nature. Most human beings are now agoraphobic; they no longer wish to venture into open spaces, to explore the universe.

Asimov indicates that some space colonization had taken place in previous centuries, but Galactic colonization has come to a standstill now that fifty worlds are inhabited. The inhabitants of the Outer Worlds are called Spacers, and they possess an advanced science of robotics. Indeed, in one world, Solaria, robots (who live on huge estates) greatly outnumber human beings who consider human contact repugnant. As we read through the tetralogy, Solaria emerges as Earth inside out and isolated. In a sense it represents another dead end for humanity because its inhabitants too have lost the drive for expansion and maintain their population artificially at sparse levels (the Solarians have advanced in the field of embryology; in the fourth novel, *Robots and Empire,* we learn that they have developed new sense organs in order to command their robots, as well as hermaphrodism).

One perceived irony of these books is that although robotics had been invented on Earth, the culmination of the science—and an economy based on robots—had taken place in the Outer Worlds, which are luxurious compared with Earth. The inhabitants of the Outer Worlds act as though robots had been born of their culture, whereas on Earth the use of robots is severely restricted, confined mainly to mines and farmlands. Only in the past quarter century, at the urgings of the Spacers, have robots slowly come into use in the Cities. On Earth there is still great hostility toward robots. A humanoid robot, such as has been developed on the planet Aurora, the oldest and most powerful of the Outer Worlds, would create panic on Earth if discovered.

Another cultural difference is that the Spacers have eliminated most human diseases and may live for hundreds of years, whereas the average lifespan of a resident of Earth is still unchanged since the twentieth century. Although they are descendants of early immigrants from Earth (the Outer Worlds had been Earth's colonies a thousand years earlier), the Spacers generally disdain Earth's crowded billions and tightly control the immigration of Earth's inhabitants to their worlds. Not least because of the threat of infectious diseases, they have established their own quarantined Spacetown near New York City, from which they communicate with it.

The powerful Spacers could exact indemnity charges from Earth on almost any pretext, and they have done so in the past. Some Spacers would go further and conquer or even destroy the Earth. Those who remember the colonial period fear that if they impose robots on Earth in order to modernize it, they will loose destruction on the Galaxy in the form of an imperialistic Earth, reborn and dangerous. We discover in *The Naked Sun* that certain fanatical Solarians are conspiring to create a robot army of conquest.

It is the Aurorans, though, who seek a peaceful and rational mediation of these contrary cultures—what they describe as C/Fe (the chemical symbols for carbon and iron, the bases of human and robot life, respectively) culture. According to the text, the diagonal line symbolizes "neither one nor the other, but a mixture of the two, without priority." In other words, C/Fe (or See-Fee) expresses a culture that combines the best of the two on an equal but parallel basis. The Aurorans—or at least those we meet in the first novel—believe that in order to remake Earth, they must abandon the isolation of Spacetown and mingle with Earthmen. In order to do so without succumbing to Earth's diseases, the Auroran Dr. Roj Nemennuh Sarton, a sociologist specializing in robotics, creates humanoid robots to live among Earthmen and gain a closer view of their lives. The first of these robots, R. Daneel Olivaw, is created in the image of Dr. Sarton (he is still functioning many thousands of years later, at the end of *Foundation and Earth*; see chapter 6).

Ultimately, the Aurorans want Earth to resume colonizing the Galaxy in order to overcome the paralysis that has seized the Outer Worlds. But like the Outer Worlds, which are themselves divided over what to do about Earth's problems, Earth itself has political factions. Prominent among them are the Medievalists, a romantic back-to-the-soil group that yearns for a return to Earth's past. It is this group that the Aurorans of Spacetown try to manipulate. When they realize that they are unable to change Earth by changing its economy (that is, by introducing robots, a development the Medievalists resist strongly), the Aurorans realize that the Medievalists are a segment of Earth's population that can be persuaded to desire what they desire. Such people, with the proper ideological conditioning (the Aurorans have in mind training schools for emigrants), will eventually turn away from Earth and return to the soil on other planets. This new social group (called Settlers in the later novels) will, they think, need robots and will either get them from the Aurorans or build their own. They will develop a C/Fe culture to suit themselves. Actually, for the most part, the Settlers do not use robots to colonize the Galaxy, but this aspect of Asimov's narrative world will be discussed later.

It seems as though the Aurorans are already practicing a variation of what later becomes the "science" of psychohistory—manipulating social groups for the benefit of mankind. Indeed, psychohistory is a dream of the foremost Auroran roboticist, Dr. Han Fastolfe, whom we first meet in *The Caves of Steel* and who is a major character in *The Robots of Dawn* (1983), which takes place on Aurora. By the end of *The Caves of Steel* the Aurorans are convinced that Earth will colonize.

We can identify the underlying "socio-logic" of the robot novels as one involving the attempted mediation of semantic contraries. This polarized semantic universe is transformed by the narrative pattern, which matches that of detective fiction. In fact, Asimov uses much of the formula of the classic detective story, which has been studied extensively by John G. Cawelti. According to

Cawelti, the classic detective formula is "perhaps the most effective fictional structure yet devised for creating the illusion of rational control over the mysteries of life."[1] Given this description, it is not surprising to find that Asimov has a strong interest in mystery and that he has written quite a few mystery stories (see *Asimov's Mysteries,* 1968). The classic detective-story formula presents us with a puzzle to be solved. Its fundamental principle is the investigation and discovery of hidden secrets, based on the moral fantasy that all problems have a clear and rational solution.

All four of Asimov's robot novels are murder mysteries involving robots either as victims (a robot is "murdered" in the *The Caves of Steel*) or as those threatened by the crime but incapable of solving it. In the first novel, the detective hero, Elijah Baley—himself an agoraphobic Earthman—is persuaded by reason that the colonization of space is the only possible salvation of Earth. In *The Naked Sun* he has to overcome his agoraphobia and solve a murder on Solaria. But the form is so ratiocinative that in the last novel, *Robots and Empire* (1985), the robots themselves conduct the investigation and, in the process, add another law to the Three Laws of Robotics (which prevent them, at least on the surface, from ever being criminals).

In cognitive terms the mystery story is very close to the science fiction story or the puzzle narrative based on normal science, which we investigated in the preceding chapter. In both patterns the supernatural is excluded as a mode of explanation, and once the secrets are revealed, they are no longer capable of disturbing or troubling us. Throughout the following discussion of narrative discourse in the robot novels, I draw upon Cawelti's clear analyses and categorizations.

## *The Caves of Steel*

According to Cawelti, the detective-story formula centers on the detective's investigation and solution of the crime. In general, the author of the mystery story will try to keep our attention focused on the process of investigation. So while the crime may be a major one with the potential for complex ramifications (the murder of an Auroran scientist in Spacetown, for example), it must not arouse too much concern for the victim and his situation.

*The Caves of Steel* (1954) does keep us coolly distant from Dr. Sarton, the murder victim, as critics such as James Gunn have noted. Near the end of the novel, Elijah ("Lije") Baley, the detective, remarks bitterly that the Aurorans had never cared who murdered Sarton; they had used the investigation as an excuse to study Earthmen under field conditions. R. Daneel

Olivaw tells Baley that although the Aurorans would like to know who committed the crime, they had never suffered any delusions about which was more important, the individual or humanity.

Asimov does, however, arouse sympathy in the reader for characters who require the detective's intervention to exonerate them (for example, Gladia Delmarre, whom Baley rescues in *The Naked Sun*). As Cawelti points out, it is not the confrontation of detective and criminal so much as the detective's rescue of the false suspects that constitutes the emotional appeal of the classic formula.

Apart from this general rule, which Asimov observes throughout the four novels, Cawelti also identifies six main phases in the narrative pattern of the classic detective story, which may not always appear in sequence and are sometimes collapsed into each other: (1) introduction of the detective, (2) crime and clues, (3) investigation, (4) announcement of the solution, (5) explanation of the solution, and (6) denouement.[2]

Initially, Asimov deviates from the formula in the way he introduces his detective hero, Lije Baley. We do not discover him ensconced in the luxury of a bachelor apartment, meditatively enjoying his meerschaum in the company of a friend (to evoke the famous Sherlock Holmes) but rather at his desk in a large bureaucracy, the Police Department of the City of New York. Baley is a forty-two-year-old married plainclothesman, and not much like the eccentric amateur sleuth often encountered in detective fiction. Baley's character gives the novel something of the atmosphere of a *roman policier*. But just to remind us (perhaps ironically) of the formula, Asimov has Baley almost immediately examine the contents of his tobacco pouch, contemplating not the intricate details of a crime but how far he can stretch the tobacco to the next quota day, if he uses it at a rate of two pipefuls a day. And Baley is not accompanied by a friend but by a somewhat pesky office-boy robot, R. Sammy, who is later "murdered."

If the opening scene has mildly comic overtones, the crime and the clues do not. Baley's boss, Commissioner Julius Enderby, tells him about the murder of a Spacer in Spacetown. (Significantly, Enderby has a number of Medievalist affectations, especially the wearing of glasses. Baley notices that his boss is wearing a new pair and is told that the old ones were broken three days ago; this later turns out to be a crucial clue to the identity of the murderer.) The victim is Dr. Roj Nemennuh Sarton, shot in the chest by a blaster.

As Cawelti indicates, a murder-mystery has two essential characteristics that have a paradoxical interrelationship. First, the crime must be surrounded by a number of tangible clues that make it absolutely clear that some agency is responsible for it; second, it must appear to be insoluble, or even to defy reason. The evidence of Sarton's corpse fulfills the first requirement; the fact that access to the murder scene from the outside is strictly controlled by the Spacers fulfills the second (it would have been impossible to smuggle a blaster through the Spacetown inspection). Moreover, although the City has unguarded exits, no City dweller would be psychologically able to endure the journey across open country to Spacetown. And because of the Three Laws of Robotics, it seems out of the question that a robot could be the murderer.

Baley is told by his boss that it is up to him to bring the murderer in on his own, but that he is going to be partnered in the investigation with one of the Spacer robots. Enderby also tells Baley that the robot must not break the case, because he could then report the human beings for incompetence. Baley's job is thus a delicate one: he must work with the robot but see that he, Baley, solves the case.

After Baley meets his robot partner, R. Daneel Olivaw, who is molded in the fair Spacer image, the pair proceed in their investigation, which has typical characteristics. That is, the investigation section of the novel (the greater part of it) presents us with a number of suspects, witnesses, and false solutions. Even Baley's wife is briefly a suspect because of a brief flirtation with a Medievalist group. False solutions are given twice in the text. Baley's first solution is that Daneel is in fact a human being, not a robot; the "corpse" was a robot; and the murder was faked for political reasons so that the Spacers could occupy Earth. But Daneel removes his arm, showing Baley the robotic construction underneath the skin, and thereby disproves that hypothesis. Later, Baley accuses Daneel of being the murderer, suggesting that he was somehow constructed without the First Law. He is proved wrong by an Earth-based robotics expert who explains to him the technical difficulties that would be involved in constructing such a robot.

At these parts of the investigation, Asimov presents us with discursive material about C/Fe culture and robotics. Dr. Fastolfe explains to Baley that no Outer World has colonized a new planet in two and a half centuries. He believes that if Earth is to survive (its political philosophy of "civism" is a dead end, in his view), there must be "a synthesis, a crossbreeding"—the building of new colonies by humans who have a City background plus the knowledge necessary to establish a C/Fe culture. At first Baley thinks this idea is nonsense, but by the end of the novel he is convinced that colonization is the only possible salvation for Earth partly because his mind has been affected by a Spacer drug intended to make him more receptive to the idea.

Included in the narrative leading to the second false solution is a lecture by Dr. Andrew Gerrigel, Earth's resident robotics expert. It turns out that a new basic theory of robotics would be required to construct a robot capable of murdering a human. An entire chapter, entitled "Words from an Expert," advances our understanding of robotics and its relationship to Heisenberg's Uncertainty Principle, which indicates that no two robot brains can be constructed exactly alike. Asimov seems to be allowing for a bit of indeterminacy to play in the context of his normal science of robotics.

In the last two chapters Baley dramatically announces the correct solution and explains how he arrived at it. Daneel is bested here; because of his logical programming, binary thinking, and quite literal belief in the benefits of C/Fe culture, he cannot see how an Earthman might have used it for at least a temporary advantage. It turns out that Enderby is the accidental murderer. An earnest Medievalist (in fact, he is one of their leaders) aware of the purpose for which Daneel had been designed, Enderby had decided to destroy him, thereby perhaps ending the Spacetown project altogether. (As Baley explains it, there is no difficulty in the notion of a robot crossing open country, even at night, alone.) Enderby had put a blaster in the robot R. Sammy's hand and instructed him to meet him at Spacetown (R. Sammy is later tricked by Enderby into committing suicide in order to destroy the evidence). Enderby had then entered Spacetown in the usual manner and been relieved of his own blaster. Once in Spacetown, he had received the other blaster from R. Sammy. Then, in the excitement of carrying out the murder, he had broken his glasses and mistaken Sarton for Daneel. After the murder he had returned the blaster to R. Sammy, who had taken it back to New York City.

Baley explains that he arrived at the correct solution through an analysis of detailed photographs taken at the scene of the crime, which reveal some slivers of glass in the grooves of the door to Sarton's house. Because of their optical properties, they are identified as bits of Enderby's broken eyeglasses, thus proving he had been at the murder scene much earlier than initially thought. Apparently, Baley deduces the rest of the solution independently from the facts of the case (although earlier Daneel had mentioned Enderby as a possible suspect because he was the one Earthman present at the scene).

In the denouement, Enderby is not taken off to jail. The Spacers agree not to prosecute him if he will maneuver the Medievalist organization in the direction of the colonization of space. This ending has the double structural advantage of linking the solution of a murder mystery and the identification of the guilty party with the goals of a science-fiction narrative. Earth is saved; mankind will colonize the Galaxy; rationality and order prevail over violence and chaos.

## *The Naked Sun*

*The Naked Sun* (1957) takes place on Solaria, which is Earth inside out. About twenty thousand Solarians inhabit the planet, together with a huge underclass of robots—two hundred million of them. The Solarians themselves are "eugenically hothoused," and almost all child rearing is done by robots because the Solarians have a taboo against personal presence. All of the Outer Worlds have a robot-based economy, but Solaria is by far the best known because of the variety and excellence of the robot models it produces. Solaria exports specialized models to all the other Outer Worlds.

Over the years Solaria has become a "villa planet," its politics based loosely on that of ancient Sparta. The Helots of this society are, of course, the robots, who can never think of revolting. So the Solarians have the advantage of a Spartan exclusiveness without any need to sacrifice themselves to developing a rigid military machine. According to their resident sociologist, Anselmo Quemot, the Solarians have also modeled themselves on the ancient Athenians in terms of cultural life. The aristocrats of Solaria seemingly live in a utopian society where the pursuit of pleasure is all.

There is one major problem, however. With little or no personal contact, the Solarians have lost insight into human nature, as well as some sciences which have strong social dimensions. In particular, they do not understand how to deal with hostility or outright violence. Hannis Gruer, Head of Solarian Security, has found out about a conspiracy to develop killer robotic spaceships—in effect, to create an army of conquest. When Gruer hears of Baley's work in solving the Spacer murder on Earth, he decides that he needs him as an adviser. He contacts the Aurorans and through them approaches the Earth government. Yet Gruer cannot persuade his own colleagues to go along with his plan until the brutal murder of Rikaine Delmarre—the first violent crime on Solaria in two centuries, and the very first murder. Delmarre—a "fetal engineer" who had been collaborating with a robotics expert named Jothan Leebig on developing a robot that could discipline children—has his skull crushed while working in his home.

Baley is sent for, and he is instructed by Undersecretary of the Justice Department Albert Minnim to find out as much as he can about Solaria (Earth's sociologists are predicting a new period of Spacer suppression—even destruction—of Earth). Baley is accompanied in his investigation by R. Daneel Olivaw, in large measure because the Aurorans also want to find out more about the secret plans of the Solarians. Daneel is mostly an observer in this story, pretending to be an Auroran human, although he does suggest possible suspects.

In the section of the book in which the crime and clues are presented, Gruer stresses the political nature of the crime to Baley and hints darkly at secret organizations on Solaria, saying that the whole human race is in danger. For his part, Baley points out the peculiarity of the case, and once again we observe a paradoxical situation. There appears to be no motive, no means (no murder weapon is found), no witnesses, and no evidence (a robot who is present at the crime becomes so disordered that it has to be scrapped). Everyone suspects Delmarre's beautiful wife, Gladia, the only person present at the scene of the crime. But before Baley can proceed very far in his conversation with Gruer, an attempt is made on Gruer's life via poison in his drink. He survives the attempt but is incapacitated for the rest of the novel. His successor as Acting Head of Security is Corwin Attlebish, a man far less disposed to listen to Baley's arguments or to aid him in his investigation.

Nonetheless—and despite the Solarians' insistence on "viewing" instead of personal interviews and his own bouts of agoraphobia (the naked sun of the title)—Baley pushes on with determination. Before his meeting with Gruer, Baley had already interviewed Gladia Delmarre. She had admitted to discovering the body after hearing her husband shout for help. The shock of the personal presence of both her husband and a dead body had caused her to faint (she had later been treated by Dr. Altim Thool, a physician and her genetic father). Despite the circumstantial evidence, she vehemently denies having committed the murder.

It is clear that we are meant to like Gladia Delmarre and to believe her. We wish to see her acquitted by Baley.[3] She is a spirited, even seductive character whom we know would thrive on human contact. By all accounts, her husband was a thoroughly cold and proper Solarian whom everyone respected but whom no one really liked (but there is never much sympathy for the victim anyway). Baley is half in love with her by the end of the novel, and they briefly become lovers in a later book. Gladia outlives Baley by a century or more, however, and becomes the heroine of *Robots and Empire*.

Baley also interviews Klorissa Cantoro, Delmarre's assistant fetologist. Because she can endure human presence and because she may be politically ambitious, she is briefly a suspect. But when she explains her genetic makeup to Baley and tells him that no one would believe her capable of murder, Baley relents. The interview with Cantoro is primarily a way for Asimov to delineate aspects of Solarian genetic engineering and to provide us with the valuable clue that Delmarre and Leebig were working on experimental robots that would have a weakened First Law and that could be instructed to discipline children without becoming mentally unstable. While Baley is visiting a group of children outside Delmarre's laboratory, an attempt is made on his life by means of a poisoned arrow. Luckily, the arrow, shot by one of the children, misses him.

Next Baley interviews Leebig, who is so fanatically prorobot and antihuman in his attitudes that we immediately suspect him of being the killer. He arrogantly lectures Baley on robotics and is infuriated when Baley proposes a theory of murder by a series of robot actions, each innocent in itself. Baley suggests that the First Law of Robotics has been misstated. It should read, "A robot may do nothing that, *to its knowledge,* will harm a human being; nor, through inaction, *knowingly* allow a human being to come to harm." Most ordinary people (the reader included, one supposes) do not realize that this is understood, but a robotics expert would. Leebig also tells Baley that Gladia hated her husband because of his coldness. When Baley interviews Gladia again, she reveals that she did quarrel with her husband often (apparently over children), but also that Leebig himself "saw" her often and commiserated, and tried hard to teach her something about robotics.

With this last information collected, it is time for the announcement of the solution. Daneel suggests that Gladia had committed the murder and that Dr. Thool, being Gladia's genetic father, had hidden the murder weapon to protect her. Baley responds by showing that it is indeed logical, but not reasonable, to think that he would have done so (this logicality is a failing of the robot mind, we are meant to conclude). Baley has his own solution and, true to the formula of the classic detective story, he calls everyone together to make a dramatic announcement (all are present by viewing, of course; the story does not violate the science-fiction conventions it has set up). Baley goes down the list of suspects and questions each on motive, opportunity, and means, eliminating the impossible until only the improbable truth remains.

Leebig, Solaria's best roboticist, had committed the murder. In love with Gladia, he had been stung when she refused to be his assistant, and he had hated Delmarre because he had refused to go along with Leebig's radical plans to create spaceships with built-in positronic brains. As a good Solarian, Delmarre had found the idea of creating a robot capable of revolting or of harming human beings repugnant. By killing Delmarre in such a way as to cast suspicion on his wife, Leebig had hoped to avenge himself on both at once. As in *The Caves of Steel,* an innocent robot—this time one with a detachable arm, which was the murder weapon—is used and later destroyed by Leebig. Leebig had instructed the robot to give Gladia its arm during a moment in which she was furious at her husband. With a weapon in her hand at the crucial moment, she had acted in a temporary blackout before either Delmarre or the robot could stop her.

Leebig breaks down hysterically at the thought that he will momentarily be put under restraint (ironically, by a robot, Daneel Olivaw, whom he thinks is human). He admits to having arranged Gruer's poisoning and the arrow meant for Baley (put in the hands of a child by a robot). He commits suicide rather than endure the approach of what he thinks is a human being.

In the denouement Gladia and Baley exchange an erotic caress of hands. She decides to emigrate to Aurora, where she can forget the entire matter and explore her newfound gregariousness. Baley returns to Earth and explains to Undersecretary Minnim the weaknesses of Solarian society, which are the same as its strengths—its robots, its low population, and the inhabitants' long lives. There is a danger that the other Outer Worlds will become Solarian some day, but Baley hopes that they will work to keep themselves in a reasonable balance and in that way remain the leaders of humankind. He asks to be sent to Aurora to find a way out of the rebellion that Earth's sociologists predict will soon happen. He argues that there may be ways for Earthmen to become Spacers themselves and colonize the Galaxy. At the end Baley finds that the City is a strange, almost alien world. He has learned to live in the naked sun.

## *The Robots of Dawn*

Asimov wrote no new robot novels for three decades after the publication of *The Naked Sun.* He had started work on a third novel set on Aurora in the mid-1950s but abandoned the project to take up science writing soon after the Russians launched Sputnik. He did not entirely abandon robotics, however. In the years that preceded the publication of *The Robots of Dawn* (1983), Asimov wrote several robot stories, notably "The Bicentennial Man," a novelette that won both a Hugo and a Nebula Award in 1977, and "Mirror Image," published in 1973 as a sequel to the Baley-Olivaw novels. Both stories are summarized in *The Robots of Dawn,* which is nearly twice as long as Asimov's previous robots novels. Because of the length of the novel form (the previous two novels were originally written for magazine serialization), Asimov was able to weave a network of intertexual correspondences between the robot novels and the Foundation series so that everything in both series happened in the same universe. Stories that are part of *I, Robot* appear as Earth legends in *The Robots of Dawn.* History is transformed into legend quite often in the later novels of the Foundation series as well.

Certainly, one narrative function of *The Robots of Dawn* is to point the robot universe in the direction of the Galactic Empire and the Foundation universe. I will point out aspects of this narrative function (we might call it "continuity fixing") as we go along. But considered as an isolated novel, *The Robots of Dawn* has the same narrative structure as the two previous robot novels. Asimov did not alter the formula, although he did incorporate more more sociological extrapolation in this novel than in anything else he had published previously. Auroran society is well imagined in concrete detail. For the purposes of this discussion, however, I will limit myself to a discussion of the novel's narrative structure and the general social dialectic it presents.

*The Robots of Dawn* unfolds in the classic puzzle pattern. Baley is summoned to Aurora to solve the puzzle of the death of a humaniform robot, Jander Panell, who has been "murdered" (there is a good deal of debate in the book about the correct terminology; Baley finally seems to settle on *roboticide,* which is a mere civil offense on Aurora). Apparently, the murderer is the robot's creator, Dr. Han Fastolfe, Aurora's greatest theoretical roboticist. From the beginning, as in the previous robot novels, the murder has serious political implications for Earth. Fastolfe is the leader of the dominant Auroran party, the Humanists, who advocate at least allowing Earth to colonize the Galaxy, if not giving them the robots to do so. If Fastolfe were to be implicated in some scandal, Earth's hopes for the future would be destroyed. Baley's task is thus not just to find the guilty party but also to exonerate Fastolfe and to save Earth.

Unfortunately, Fastolfe seems to have already confessed to the crime when Baley arrives on Aurora. Joining forces again with Baley is R. Daneel Olivaw, along with another robot created by Fastolfe (though not a humaniform one), Giskard Reventlov, who generally remains in the background. Jander, the second humaniform robot ever created (Daneel was the first) was destroyed not by violence but by a subtle verbal program that induced a mental "freeze-out." The paradox of the crime is that only Fastolfe, with his advanced knowledge of robotics, is capable of creating such a program. His possible motives, not revealed until later in the novel, basically involve the destruction of his own creation in order to discredit the idea of a robot colonization of the Galaxy (what his political enemies, the Globalists, want). Fastolfe has refused to make any further humaniform robots (he had collaborated with Dr. Sarton on Daneel, but Jander is entirely his own creation), because he thinks Aurora, like Solaria, is heading toward complete dependence on robots. Were Fastolfe to die, the new science of humaniformics, which Asimov links to psychohistory, would die with him.

Since Fastolfe denies having committed the crime, the only other possibility seems to be that the robot's demise was due to random chance—perhaps a spontaneous event in the positronic flow along the brain paths. Fastolfe himself admits that this is of extremely low probability. But although "the pure uncertainty of positronic drift" is most likely not the solution, Fastolfe stubbornly adheres to it as correct.

Baley begins an investigation that uncovers the sexual codes of Aurora, as well as a tangled web of hidden desires that exist despite the society's official toleration of promiscuity. Fastolfe takes Baley to the former Gladia Delmarre, now Gladia Solaria. Jander had been given to her as a "gift"—probably, it is suggested, in order to satisfy her sexually. A humaniform robot, Jander had been completely capable of engaging in sexual intercourse, and because of the First Law he was more than capable of pleasing a woman. Gladia had soon fallen in love with him; she tells Baley that she remembers Jander as her husband.

During the eight months in which Jander was with her, Gladia had been pursued by Santirix Gremionis, a "personnel artist," who had offered himself to her several times, despite her consistent refusals. Gremionis had been madly in love with Vasilia Aliena, a roboticist who is also Fastolfe's genetic daughter. Vasilia hates her father, however, and has remained virginal ever since he refused to have sexual relations with her (what on Earth would be incest). She had suggested Gladia to Gremionis as a substitute for herself, since there is a strong physical resemblance between them.

One hypothesis that Baley arrives at is that there had been a conspiracy between Vasilia and Gremionis, motivated by Gremionis's jealousy of Jander. Another is that Jander had become unbalanced because of his awareness of the shame Gladia felt in taking him as a husband (although Gladia admits to no shame). Vasilia suggests another solution. Because Jander, like Daneel, had been created as models to solve the problem of the human brain, Jander had been given to Gladia and then destroyed by Fastolfe as part of a monstrous experiment.

What seems to be the correct solution comes after Baley interviews Kelden Amadiro, head of the Robotics Institute, which had been set up in opposition to Fastolfe. Amadiro is the leader of the Globalists, who want humaniform robots to colonize the Galaxy, creating new worlds in the image of Aurora. He believes that Fastolfe is trying to make humaniform robots appear less useful than they are. For his part, Fastolfe believes that robot colonization of the Galaxy would be catastrophic for Aurora and for humanity. Humans will never have left home, he argues; they will simply have another, newer world, exactly like Aurora, in which to continue their decay. Baley forces a political compromise on Amadiro—the Globalists will have to agree to allow all of the other Spacer worlds, as well as Earth, to have freedom of settlement in the Galaxy—when he reveals that Amadiro is most probably Jander's murderer.

Amadiro had been after the secret of the humaniform robot, which the Robotics Institute had been unable to discover. Daneel, as part of Dr. Fastolfe's establishment, could not easily be reached. Jander, on the other hand, had been part of Gladia's establishment, and Gladia was not sophisticated in protecting robots. While Gladia was out walking with Gremionis one day, Amadiro had taken the opportunity to converse with Jander—possibly by tridimensional viewing—with the intention of studying his responses and then erasing any sign of the visit. Amadiro accidentally immobilized Jander during this process and committed roboticide.

This solution is accepted by all parties before the Chairman of the Auroran Legislature. But in a surprise ending (although in retrospect one realizes that Asimov does provide some clues earlier), Baley finds out, in a conversation with Giskard, that Giskard had killed Jander. Because of an accident in his programming—caused, ironically, by Vasilia in her youth—Giskard can read minds and can also "push" people mentally in certain directions. In fact, he had obscured Baley's mind on several occasions during the investigation in order to test the mettle of Earthmen. Giskard, a true disciple of Fastolfe, wants Earthmen to settle the Galaxy—but alone, without the help of robots of any kind. He believes that humans will be much better off solving problems on their own, although he holds out the possibility that robots may secretly want to intervene again in the distant future (Asimov thus leaves open a narrative option that he later takes up in *Prelude to Foundation*).

Furthermore, Giskard claims to be able to program other robots to be like himself (which he does to Daneel at the end of *Robots and Empire*). This is believable because he had been able to immobilize Jander when Amadiro got too close to working out the method for designing a true humaniform robot. He had also "pushed" Fastolfe to send for Baley in the first place and had put into the scientist's mind an obsession with psychohistory and the Laws of Humanics, which Fastolfe thinks of as the equivalent of the Three Laws of Robotics.

Although Asimov seems locked into the idea of an all-human Galaxy because of what he has already written in the Foundation series, Fastolfe in this novel expresses the fear that more energetic alien intelligences may conquer the Galaxy before humans do—an idea that appears to be the basis for much of the narrative in the latest of the Foundation novels (see chapter 6). Giskard allows Baley to remember all that he has deduced about him, but "pushes" him so that he does not have the slightest desire to share that information.

In *The Robots of Dawn,* Asimov ties up some major threads of narrative continuity and opens others. In this novel he explains how the far end of his Galactic Empire, with its short-lived humans and non–robot-based culture, developed out of the Spacer society depicted in the two robot novels. He also explains what happened to the idea of C/Fe culture, which Fastolfe was so keen on in *The Caves of Steel.* In addition (and perhaps most interestingly), Asimov links the science of robotics with the science of psychohistory, which dominates the Foundation novels. He accomplishes all this through the ingenious use of the character Giskard, a telepathic robot who does not appear to be complex in design. Yet Giskard undoubtedly suggested Fastolfe's seeming change of mind, as well as the concept of the future science of psychohistory, which Giskard tells Baley is necessary now that the long-lived robotized culture of the Spacer worlds is coming to an end.

After *The Robots of Dawn,* Asimov had yet to deal with the concept of a radioactive earth (which he had established in the Galactic Empire novels) in order to link all his novels together in one narrative universe. This issue is addressed in *Robots and Empire.*

## *Robots and Empire*

This last of the robot novels (so far), published in 1985, is set two hundred years after *The Robots of Dawn* and takes place on Aurora, Solaria, Earth, and the oldest of the Settler worlds, Baleyworld. Asimov tells the story of most of the intervening years by means of analepses that occur in the minds of the robots Daneel and Giskard, who have perfect memories, and Gladia Solaria, who is now 233 years old.

In the intervening years much had happened to Gladia, and much had not. She had met Baley again five years after the end of *The Robots of Dawn,* when Baley was an immigrant to one of the Settler worlds. They had had a brief love affair, after which they never saw each other again. Gladia later had a son, Darrel, who may have been fathered by Baley. Possibly to cope with the boredom of a long life alone, Gladia had married again, this time to Gremionis. When her friend Dr. Han Fastolfe had died, he had left Giskard and Daneel to her for her protection, and these robots live with her.

Although Baley had died at the age of seventy-nine, he is still very much alive, as something of a prophet, in the minds of Gladia, Giskard, and Daneel. His predictions about a period of crisis in the colonization of the Galaxy are basic to the plot.

Dr. Kelden Amadiro, Fastolfe's rival at the Robotics Institute, is still alive and scheming the destruction or downfall of Earth with Vasilia and a new character, Levular Mandamus. Amadiro is bitter about the failure of the Institute's line of humanoid robots, which had been designed with the help of Fastolfe, who had reached a compromise with his enemies at the end of *The Robots of Dawn.* These humanoid robots had just not been wanted in Auroran society. Aurorans had claimed to give robots nearly equal rights and had not objected to robot-human sex in theory, but they had demurred at actually allowing the latter to happen. Neither Auroran men nor Auroran women had wanted to compete with humanoid robots like Jander. Although the Institute had labored to explain that the humanoid robots were intended not as inhabitants of Aurora but as pioneers who would colonize new, habitable planets for Aurorans, suspicions and objections had fed on themselves until the Institute had to abandon the project—though not before some of the robots had been built (later to be mothballed) by Amadiro.

Fastolfe had hoped for a healthy competition between Earthmen and the Spacers in colonizing the Galaxy, but all the alternatives to using humanoid robots had come to nothing. The Spacers—superior, self-absorbed, and dependent on robots—will not travel to rude and unformed worlds; nor do they like humaniform robots. As a result, the Aurorans had done little to colonize the Galaxy. Nor had they been able to sell their robots to Solaria, mysteriously abandoned by humans.

The short-lived Earthmen have become the dominant force in Galactic colonization, provoking a crisis that Baley had foreseen. The fear of Spacer retaliation is high among the Settler worlds, and *Robots and Empire* involves a conspiracy to destroy the Earth by making its crust radioactive. The exact nature of the plot against Earth (it involves the placement of nuclear intensifiers at key points on the Earth's surface by humanoid robots secreted on Earth and reactivated by Amadiro) is not revealed until the end of the novel. We must guess at it from clues supplied in the narrative as the robot detectives, Giskard and Daneel, proceed with their investigation along with their human partners.

In the third chapter Gladia is visited by a seventh-generation Settler descendant of Baley, Daneel Giskard Baley. He is a Trader who wants to exploit the situation on Solaria by appropriating the robots that have been left behind and selling them to the other Spacer worlds. Since Gladia is the only known Solarian left in the Galaxy, D. G. Baley hopes that she will accompany him and be able to control the robots. Gladia has no real reason to go, but as Vasilia later deduces, she is probably "pushed" by Giskard, who wants to remove himself from Aurora because he realizes that Vasilia is very close to discovering that he has telepathic abilities.

D. G. Baley, Gladia, and the two robots travel to Solaria (in *Foundation and Earth* we find out that the human inhabitants had moved underground), now controlled by robot overseers, who attack the Trader ship. They soon leave the planet and proceed to Baleyworld, where Gladia, ("pushed" by Giskard) makes a rousing speech in favor of peace in the Galaxy, a cause to which she has decided to devote her life.

The plot in this part of the novel mainly concerns the attempts of Amadiro and Vasilia to recover Gladia, but the real object of interest is Giskard. Vasilia has convinced Amadiro that Giskard is a telepathic robot—a powerful weapon if they can control him. Vasilia does not know that Mandamus has already devised a plan for Earth's destruction.

Giskard eventually erases Gladia's memory and leaves for Earth with her and Daneel. Gladia, having proclaimed herself a citizen of the Galaxy, plans to address Earth in the same manner she did Baleyworld, but an attempt is made on her life. Actually, it is a disguised attempt on Giskard's life by one of Amadiro's humaniform robots. Soon the robots locate the headquarters of the conspirators on Earth (appropriately, on Three Mile Island). In a surprise ending, Giskard, seemingly obeying the First Law, neutralizes Daneel and allows Mandamus to succeed.

The nuclear intensifiers will steadily and irreversibly increase the natural radioactivity of the Earth's crust over the next century and a half, until certain areas of the planet are unlivable. This will destroy the social structure of Earth; the mystical abode and origin of humanity—the source of Settler emotional strength—will be obliterated. But this seeming catastrophe is, in Giskard's view, ultimately a good thing. He argues with Daneel that the mystique of Earth may have eventually impeded human development, just as the mystique of robots and long life had hobbled the progress of the Spacers. Earth will now streak outward into the Galaxy at a redoubled pace, and, he says, "without Earth to look back to always, without Earth to set up a god of the past, [human beings] will establish a Galactic Empire." It is clearly suggested however, that in this new, demystified future, humankind must develop a science to guide itself—psychohistory—and the robots now face the task of helping humanity to develop it.

The plot of *Robots and Empire* thus ends with the crisis averted. Though Asimov was unable to do away with the radioactive Earth he had described in his Galactic Empire novels, he made it a functional part of an ongoing narrative universe. Strictly speaking, *Robots and Empire* is not a murder mystery in the classic sense; it is more like the Foundation novels, in which an unknown is searched for, sometimes by two or more groups of characters (e.g., the search for the location of the Second Foundation in the Foundation novels, or the search for the lost Earth itself). Nonetheless, the novel does present a seeming paradox, which the robots have to overcome.

They know early on that something sinister is alive in the minds of Amadiro and Mandamus; they even suspect that the fate of billions on Earth and throughout the rest of the Galaxy may depend on their finding out what it is. But that is just their problem. The Three Laws of Robotics are stated in such a way that the robots can only deal with individual human beings, not with the human aggregate. They cannot interfere with the plans of Mandamus and Amadiro, no matter what they find out, for fear of harming them. As Giskard phrases it: "We are left with the certainty of a deadly crisis coming, but a crisis whose nature we do not know, and cannot find out, and which we are therefore helpless to counter."

Daneel's memory of Baley finally helps the robots resolve the paradox. They do so by creating a new Law of Robotics, the Zeroth Law, which transcends the First Law. When Baley had been about to die, he had attempted to protect Daneel by telling him that he, Baley, was just one thread in the immense tapestry of human life being woven by Spacer and Earthman alike. In such a context the individual does not matter. Daneel reasons that since Baley's words did protect him in that crisis, the Three Laws are incomplete.

The Zeroth Law takes precedence: "a robot must not injure humanity or, through inaction, allow humanity to come to harm." Daneel, who thinks more like a human being, is finally able to convince Giskard to accept the transcendence of the First Law by pointing out that Giskard's own studies of human history—his search for the Laws of Humanics, or techniques for predicting and guiding human history—already deal with "the human tapestry." Giskard finally accepts this line of reasoning,—that Robots must act for the greater good of humanity—though not without some agonizing. In the end, the strain on his circuits is too much for him. He expires, but not before passing on his telepathic abilities to Daneel by telling him which pathway in his positronic brain makes such abilities possible.

In effect, by understanding their own minds, the robots themselves become roboticists. Two sciences, robotics and psychohistory, the latter now seeming to be a logical outgrowth of the former, are woven into the one large tapestry that is the Asimovian universe.

# *Chapter Five*
# The Galactic Empire Novels

## *The Stars, Like Dust*

With the last of the robot novels, Asimov had perhaps resolved the paradox that an Earth that had committed radioactive suicide could be the origin of a Galactic civilization. I say perhaps because in *The Stars, Like Dust* (1951), the first of the Galactic Empire novels, Earth is indeed radioactive (and has been for a thousand years), but the radioactivity is attributed to a nuclear war. Of course, we could suppose that the increasing radioactivity of the Earth's crust, due to the secret machinations of the Aurorans, both robots and humans (see chapter 4), may have led to the outbreak of a nuclear confrontation between nations. But Asimov has not yet written a story that entirely resolves this issue of continuity in his narrative world.

Most of the action in *The Stars, Like Dust* does not take place on Earth but in the Nebular Kingdoms of the Galaxy, near the famous Horsehead Nebula. All the characters, however, know that Earth is the original home of humanity (by the time of the first Foundation novel, *Prelude to Foundation,* this knowledge has been lost). Humankind has just begun to settle the first few thousand worlds of the millions that are potentially habitable. Robots are present, but only in the background, as servants. No Galactic Era (G.E.) dates are given, as they are in some of the later novels. Trantor, the seat of the Galactic Empire during its glory and fall, is never mentioned.

Politically, it is a time of small stellar kingdoms trying to establish their hegemony over others. One such kingdom, Tyrann, the 1,099th settled by man over seven hundred years ago, had begun to spread its control militarily, having conquered some fifty planets. Tyrann's control had been arrested thirty years ago, however, by the planet Lingane. Other planets of the Nebular Kingdoms that are mentioned, such as Rhodia and Nephelos, are outright vassals of the Tyranni. Lingane, however, has retained a degree of autonomy. It remains an Associated State, theoretically the equal "ally" of Tyrann.

The political maneuverings of these two powers drive the story. The villain of the piece is Sander Jonti, Autarch of Lingane, who in a bid for power decides to destroy one of the leaders of the resistance to the Tyranni, the Rancher of Widemos, by betraying him. The Rancher is consequently executed as a traitor. Biron Farrill, the Rancher's son, is the hero of the novel. He wants to avenge his father's death, but he does not know of Jonti's role in his father's death—and neither does the reader—until late in the story. The resistance knows of a strange Rebellion World, and of a precious document, taken from Earth, that would be very dangerous to the power of the Tyranni.

On the discourse level the novel unfolds as a quest for Rebellion World and for the document by three groups of people. One group consists of Farrill; Artemisia, daughter of Hinrik, Director of Rhodia (Hinrik plays weakling madman to the Tyranni while actually being the leader of the resistance); and Gillbret, Artemisia's uncle. The second group is led by Commissioner Simok Aratap of Tyrann, who must find Rebellion World in order to protect his government. The third group, comprises the Autarch and his minions, initially appear to be on the side of Farrill and Artemisia, who is fleeing to escape a dreaded political marriage. But the Autarch himself has designs on Artemisa and wins her away from Farrill by telling him that her father murdered the Rancher of Widemos.

All three groups visit planets in the Horsehead nebula in search of Rebellion World, and this activity accounts for much of the incidental scientific details in the novel. Eventually the Autarch's bid for power is exposed to Aratap and he is killed by one of his own men. Gillbret gives his life in an apparently successful attempt to mislead Aratap into believing that there is no Rebellion World. However, in an ending reminiscent of Poe's famous detective story, "The Purloined Letter," we discover that we have already visited Rebellion World; it is somewhere within the Rhodian system. As Hinrik explains, there are two ways to hide and object: put it where no one can find it (within the Horsehead Nebula), or put it in plain sight, where no one would ever think of looking for it. Hinrik had opted for the latter.

The purloined document turns out to be none other than the Constitution of the United States of America, which enunciates the principle that the governed should govern. Hinrik explains that this document will destroy Tyrann, as well as the other kingdoms, such as Lingane, but it will save the Nebular Kingdoms. Without it the resistance could perhaps have defeated the Tyranni, but they would only have exchanged one form of despotism for another: "We and they must both be delivered into the ashcan of outmoded political systems." Thus, the political theme of this novel of intrigue (Asimov calls it an interstellar romance) is the democratic principle that people should govern themselves.

In an introduction to *The Stars, Like Dust,* and in *The Currents of Space,* which is discussed next, Asimov points out that in these two novels (in contrast to the Smith-Campbell romances—popular with an earlier generation of readers—which were primarily us-against-the-natives adventure stories), the natural superiority of one group over another is never invoked—not even as an unspoken assumption.[1] Indeed, the Tryanni will not be defeated because they are in some way now inferior to the resistance.

Interestingly, the Tyranni character Aratap is in many ways the most sympathetic and well-rounded character in the book. At least one critic has found in him many of Asimov's personal characteristics, not the least of which is a love of rational order and pattern. The novel remains Asimov's least favorite, however, because the business of the secret document was forced on him by his editor, Horace Gold. Finally, it should be noted that these democratic hopes for the Galaxy in *The Stars, Like Dust* are not borne out by latter novels in the series.

## *The Currents of Space*

In this novel, published in 1952, Trantor has emerged as a major power in the Galaxy, although it is not yet a Galactic Empire. The Trantorian Republic had been a mere five worlds five hundred years earlier, but had become a Confederation and then an Empire containing half of the inhabited worlds in the Galaxy, including Earth. It is now poised on the brink of conversion to a Galactic Empire. Presumably, this development would result in a universal peace—*pax Trantorica.* But the Galaxy's second-richest planet after Trantor, Sark, stands in the way. Trantor controls half a million worlds, yet its wealth only matches that of Sark, which controls Florina, a planet on which kyrt, the most valuable substance in the Galaxy, grows. Kyrt is a versatile miracle fiber that has numerous industrial properties and artistic applications. Because it grows only on Florina, export of the item is a source of vast wealth for the Sarkites, who exploit the colonials both genetically and economically.

Each year they skim the cream of Florina's youth from the planet's fields and villages. The selected individuals are taken to Sark for training as Townmen (native governors for the towns). Those who prove mediocre are retained as clerical assistants. Neither the Townmen nor the clerical assistants may breed without losing their positions; thus the best of the Florinian genes are continually withdrawn from circulation.

The political intrigue between Sark and Trantor (which maintains an embassy on Sark) and the impending destruction of Florina provide the background and much of the action of the story—which, as usual in Asimov, takes the form of a mystery.

Before examining that mystery, however, we should note that Asimov postulates the development of a new science, Spatio-analysis, in this novel. Spatio-analysis is the study of the arrangement of elements in various regions of space. The elements wind through space like currents (hence the title of the novel). Knowledge of how these currents are arranged might explain how the universe was created and how it developed (in fact, Asimov postulates a theory of supernova formation based on the carbon current of space).

The new science requires a certain breed of scientist—one who is happy in space for long periods of time. As it happens, nearly a third of all Spatio-analysts are recruited from one planet, Earth. Anyone who has grown up on such a radioactive world is bound to feel a certain amount of fear and anxiety about planets—or so Asimov reasons—and thus will feel safe only in space. Most people seem to consider these scientists borderline psychotics anyway. Their motto is the somewhat wry "We analyze Nothing."

The main character of *The Currents of Space* is Rik, a Spatio-analyst from Earth. The mystery of the story surrounds him and why his memory has been destroyed. Before this happens, he broadcasts a message to the local Interstellar Spatio-analytic Bureau indicating that the planet Florina is in great danger. We learn later that Florina's sun is in the pre-nova stage, and that its passage through the carbon current of space will have a catalytic effect, making the star a nova. Thus the "Mysterious Case of the Psycho-probed Earthman," as one character phrases it, has three aspects: (1) What is the danger that threatens Florina, or, rather, the entire Galaxy? (2) Who was the person who had psycho-probed the Earthman? (3) Why had the person used the psycho-probe?

As usual in an Asimovian mystery, there are several reconstructions of events, and the true version emerges at the end. Most of the novel is taken up with the various versions of events (there are also three murders in the course of the story) and the political intrigues that might surround them. For example, the Squire of Fife, one of the most powerful men on Sark, believes that the motive for the crimes is blackmail on the part of his political rivals. The blackmailer X, (variously postulated to be the Squire of Trantor or one of the other Great Squires), had at some point learned of Rik's message that Florina is in danger. Although X probably considers the warning a mad story, X finds that the concept of currents of space makes an excellent propaganda tool. If the Squire of Fife does not give in to his demands, X intends to force a surrender by disrupting Florinian production of kyrt through rumors of destruction.

As it turns out, the Squire of Fife is wrong only about the identity of his blackmailer—the Townman Myrlyn Terens, a Florinian educated on Sark for the civil service, and a character with whom we are familiar from the outset of the novel. Terens hates the Sarkites and had long sought a way to destroy them. When he was a temporary traffic manager at a spaceport, a year before the novel opens, he had intercepted Rik's message. Presenting himself to Rik as the Squire of Fife in the ironic belief that Rik would talk openly because he believed Fife was anxious to do whatever was best for Florina, Terens got Rik to explain the story behind the warning. He had later found it difficult to control Rik and therefore had used a psycho-probe on him. Unfortunately, Terens had underestimated the depth of Rik's anxiety and probed too deep, rendering him mindless. Terens had disposed of Rik by putting him in the care of Valona March, a Florinian peasant girl. He had felt sure that Rik's memory would return and that he, Terens, would still need Rik's knowledge. Besides, if he had killed Rik, Terens would have forfeited the good will of Trantor and the Interstellar Spatio-analytic Bureau, with which he wants to ally himself. By sending blackmail letters to the Squire of Fife, Terens hopes to take control of enough of the kyrt lands to gain the leverage make a deal with Trantor on his own terms and force the Sarkites off the planet. Of course, Terens's plan cannot really succeed; by carrying it out, he would merely be exchanging one master for another. But he continues anyway, and after committing a series of murders to hide himself, he is tracked down by police.

Asimov arrives at a better solution to the nasty business of Sarkite-Florinian political rivalry and exploitation by having Rik remember the details of his theory of what induces a sun to become a supernova. Aided by his colleague, Dr. Selim Junz, Rik explains that Florina's sun has moved into an area of space rich in carbon currents. This will boost the star's radiation tremendously. What is more, since twenty novas occur every year, the entire Galaxy will be affected, not just one planet. Trantor must help evacuate Florina, for if it does not, other planets in danger will know that when their time comes the Empire will not aid them. With Trantor putting its responsibility to the people of the Galaxy above the maintenance of mere property rights, it will win good will that it could never win by force. The people of the Galaxy will be the victors. In another twist on Rik's theory, it seems that cheap kyrt will be available throughout the Galaxy as well. What is ordinary cotton elsewhere is kyrt on Florina because of radiation factors induced in a prenova stellar system, which can now be duplicated anywhere.

The argument presented by Rik and Junz appears to convince Ludigan Abel, the Trantorian ambassador, and in an epilogue set a year later, the evacuation is well under way. Terens decides to go down with his planet, however. Rik and Valona decide to return to Earth, which many people now doubt is the original planet of the human race. Because Rik is an Earthman, he does not want Earth to be abandoned. Together they vow to work to change its surface back to what it had once been.

On the discourse level, this book—which consists of flashbacks that seem only to catch us up with the present—is one of Asimov's more difficult novels to follow. Critics have rightly complained about its narrative technique. I can only suggest, in concordance with Joseph Patrouch, that Asimov was perhaps attempting to represent the operation of a disturbed memory.[2] Also, the phrase *currents of a story* is used in at least one passage, and this suggests that Asimov may have been trying to link the unfolding of a scientific theory with the process of narration. But these are only guesses. The novel awaits a detailed analysis that accounts for its narrative technique in terms of the transformation of story into discourse.

## *Pebble in the Sky*

*Pebble in the Sky* (1950), Asimov's last Galactic Empire novel (although chronologically his first novel published) is set almost entirely on Earth in the year 827 G.E., before the Empire's decline (which is chronicled in the Foundation series). The story is unusual for Asimov in that it does not revolve around a major mystery. To be sure, there are numerous plots and subplots—and we are kept from knowing too much about them—but the details of the main plot are revealed to us about halfway through the novel: Earth, a planet now despised an outcast by the rest of the Galaxy because of its radioactivity, plans to exact revenge on the Empire by spreading a disease called Common Fever, which is harmless to Earthmen but fatal to Outsiders. In short, Earth plans to wage biological warfare. The remainder of the novel concerns attempts to stop Earth's Zealots from carrying out their plan and exacting payment from the Empire for the antitoxin.

This main plot involves an interesting assortment of characters (and perhaps the novel itself is a novel of character, as James Gunn has suggested). First there is the sixty-two-year-old retired tailor Joseph Schwartz, who is transported from the year 1949 to an Earth thousands of years in the future by means of a freak radioactive accident. The much-confused Schwartz is taken in by a farming family, who hope to use him to help fulfill their work quota and to save the wife's father, Grew, who has suffered paralysis of the legs and will soon be due for euthanasia at the age of sixty.

In order to improve Schwartz's mental capacities, the family takes him to a scientist named Affret Shekt, who has invented a device called a Synapsifier. This device improves the quickness and effectiveness of thought. After treatment with the Synapsifier, Schwartz finds his mind much improved. He learns the contemporary Earth language quickly, and the text features in detail the moves of a chess game that Schwartz plays with Grew. Slowly, however, Schwartz becomes aware of new mental powers—the Mind Touch, as he calls them. He learns that he can read minds, immobilize others, and even kill. These mental powers become crucial to the resolution of the plot.

Unbeknownst to the family, Shekt's invention has gotten him enmeshed in the Common Fever plot. A secret cabal called the Society of the Ancients has been forcing Shekt to use the Synapsifier to improve the minds of their biological scientists, who have come up with the means for biological warfare. The leader of this cabal, Balkis, is the secretary to the High Minister of Earth—a scheming, paranoid character who looks for hidden motives behind every action. Balkis has his agents watching many people. As soon as he learns of Schwartz's Synapsifier treatment, he is quick to combine that knowledge with certain other facts to produce a theory that the Empire is conspiring to destroy Earth.

Meanwhile, Bel Arvardan, a distinguished young archaeologist from the planet Baronn in the Sirius Sector (which is Earth's sector as well), is visiting Earth under Imperial sponsorship. His mission is to gather evidence to support a theory of human evolution that contradicts accepted scientific beliefs. Arvardan believes that humanity originated on some single planet and radiated by degrees throughout the Galaxy. The textbooks of the day, however, present an orthodox archaeology that posits the evolution of human types independently on various planets, followed by a merger of these various strains. (Interestingly, we learn that Arvardan had previously written a monograph on Rigellian robot culture, a hint at the robot novels). Because of the prevailing prejudices against Earth, which is seen as a barbarous, filthy, ritualistic, and rebellious world (Asimov is drawing a broad historical parallel with the perception of ancient Rome in Judea), Balkis is having a difficult time convincing others of the truth of his beliefs—and particularly Ennius, Procurator of Earth. Arvardan has asked Ennius for permission to visit Earth's forbidden radioactive areas for scientific purposes, and Ennius has passed this request on to Earth's High Minister. It is knowledge of this request that prompts the conspiracy theory of Balkis.

In Balkis's paranoid mind, which looks for patterns and symmetries, Arvardan is a "queer mirror image" of Schwartz. Arvardan in not unknown, like Schwartz, but a famous figure; not an inconspicuous visitor, but one who arrives on Earth with lots of publicity. Because of these symmetries, Balkis thinks that Schwartz is an Outsider agent on Earth, that Shekt is the contact man with the Assimilationist traitors (i.e., those who want to become normal citizens of the Empire) among Earth's population of twenty million, and that Arvardan is the contact man with the Empire. Balkis even suspects Pola, Shekt's daughter, of being part of the this Assimilationist conspiracy.

As Asimov presents it, Balkis's conspiracy theory is clearly recognizable as the product of his paranoia—that is, the reader is not left to guess whether or not it is true, as is generally the case in Asimov's novels. Nonetheless, Balkis fulfills an important narrative function in this novel that must be performed when a mystery is at the center of the plot. Balkis presents alternative interpretations of events—counternarrative or even antinarrative programs. As Joseph Patrouch observes, in Asimov's novels there always seems to be a character whose function it is to second-guess or criticize Asimov's own plotting, and who indeed often comes up with solutions that are more intellectually satisfying than the one Asimov ultimately offers.[3]

Of course, none of what Balkis believes about Arvardan is true. At least on the surface, Arvardan believes himself to be free of prejudices against Earth people. And it is not long before Arvardan becomes romantically involved with an Earthwoman, Pola Shekt, though their romance is disrupted for a while when she learns he is an Outsider.

Several events lead to the end of the novel. Schwartz sets off for Chica (Chicago) in order to avoid the forthcoming census and death. In spite of the Mind Touch, however, he is captured. Meanwhile, Arvardan learns of the plot against the Empire from Pola and her father but is unable to do much about it. Eventually they are all captured by Balkis, who envisions himself as the new ruler of the Galaxy. Schwartz manages to escape and Mind-Touches an Imperial Officer whose mind is full of hatred for Earth people, causing him to bomb the Temple of Senloo (St. Louis), where the virus and the missiles that will spread it are housed. Thereby Schwartz—an unlikely hero for a science-fiction novel in the first place—saves the Galaxy, even though it is clear that he is sympathetic with the plight of oppressed Earth people.

In this novel the Empire clearly stands for enlightenment. If it had not been so, Asimov makes clear, rebellious Earth would have been bloodily erased from the roll of inhabited planets long ago. It is also clear that although there is an Emperor on Trantor, the early Empire allows conquered worlds cultural autonomy, and the Galactic government has become a representative one. We are led to feel that choosing to side with the Empire, as Schwartz does, is the only rational and humane way in which to settle Earth's grievances. The despotic theocracy that Balkis and the Zealots would have set up would have destroyed millions of innocent lives.

At the end, rich Trantor sends huge convoys carrying normal soil to Earth in an attempt to remake the planet. But the Earthmen themselves will be doing the work, making the desert bloom in the hope that one day Earth will be a planet among planets, "looking all humanity in the eye with dignity and equality." (One cannot help but think of the state of Israel, which proclaimed independence little more than a year before *Pebble in the Sky* was published.) In this manner Asimov's narrative universe is linked with the Enlightenment narrative of the progress of reason and the critique of prejudice (see chapter 7).

## *Chapter Six*

# The Foundation Novels

## *Prelude to Foundation*

As Thomas Kuhn points out, it is only during periods of normal science, when scientists are working in concert within an accepted paradigm, that progress seems obvious and assured. For example, throughout the preparadigm period, when there is a multiplicity of competing schools of thought, evidence of progress (except within schools) is very hard to find. What is more, in the postparadigm period, when confronted with anomaly or crisis, scientists take a different attitude toward paradigms, and the nature of their research changes accordingly. In these periods of extraordinary science, as Kuhn calls them, the scientist in crisis may generate speculative theories, design "thought experiments," or be willing to try almost anything: "He will, in the first place, often seem a man searching at random, trying experiments just to see what will happen, looking for an effect whose nature he cannot quite guess."[1] Kuhn goes on to note that this fits our most prevalent cultural image of the scientist.

*Prelude to Foundation* (1988) gives us something very like this image in the young Hari Seldon, a thirty-two-year-old Outworld mathematician who at the outset of the novel has come to Trantor, the capital of the Empire, to attend the Decennial Convention and present his paper on psychohistory. Soon after presenting his paper, he is ensnared in a web of political intrigue cast by those who want to make use of his remarkable theory of prediction—though it soon becomes evident that they do not understand its limitations.

*Prelude to Foundation* also tells of the quest to found a new science, psychohistory, on the possibility that there is a "mathematics of history" that would permit the description of the natural laws of society (the Laws of Humanics) in such a way as to make it possible to anticipate the future with a substantial degree of probability. This quest aspect of the book, in which Seldon must find a device or model to simplify psychohistory (as he says, "a mathematical trick or a historical trick or something totally imaginary"—in other words, a thought experiment), relates the ideas in the book most clearly to those of Kuhn. Seldon had proved that psychohistory was at least theoretically possible in a paper, but what he now needs is a means to carry out experiments—a "working technique of psychohistory." Meanwhile, as mentioned early in the novel and reiterated throughout, normal science and technological advance are declining in the Empire. Most scientists in the year 12,020 G.E. have rigidified into a stance that automatically condemns any speculation. All these things contribute to the idea that *Prelude to Foundation* takes place in a period of crisis, when extraordinary science is in evidence and is perhaps needed.

Seldon has to be motivated to turn theory in practice, however, for initially he does not believe it possible or even see why it is necessary. This is accomplished by one of the most ingenious twists in the Asimovian universe. After an early interview with the current Emperor, Cleon I, in which Seldon expresses the view that psychohistory is impractical (he admits that he lacks the historical knowledge that might give human meaning to his "elegant equations in innumerable unknowns"), he is interviewed by Chetter Hummin, who professes to be a journalist. Hummin tells Seldon of a "downward spiral" in the affairs of the Galaxy and, after they dispose of a couple of thugs who accost them in a public park, of the scheming of Eto Demerzel, the Emperor's Chief of Staff, who has probably sent the thugs to capture Seldon. Hummin is a very persuasive person, and soon he has Seldon enlisted in the cause of saving humankind and the Galaxy by developing a practical psychohistory. Evidently he also has many powerful political connections; before long he has Seldon safely (or so he thinks) ensconced on the campus of one of Trantor's better schools, Streeling University, where he can do his research and be looked after by Dors Venabili, a woman historian.

From the outset we notice something not quite human about Hummin. He is almost too strong and too persuasive, and somehow too idealistic, to be a real human being. In fact, he is none other than R. Daneel Olivaw, who also plays the role of the seeming villian of the piece, Eto Demerzel. This is not revealed until the end of the novel, although in retrospect one realizes that there are some broad hints throughout—especially the reverent way in which Hummin always refers to The Laws of Humanics. He also rescues Seldon a little too easily from his scrapes with authority. In short, he seems to have a foreknowledge about the outcome of certain events, and a capacity to influence them, that is beyond the human. He even guides Seldon through a series of attempts to found psychohistory, all of which take place on different sectors of Trantor, which is made up of over eight hundred sectors.

The first sector is the university, a place supposedly free from the Emperor's power. Here Seldon embarks on a program of research to learn more about the history of the Galaxy. He particularly wants to learn about its early history, in which human social interactions would have taken place on a simpler scale than they do in the Empire's current twenty-five million inhabited worlds. Unfortunately, Seldon soon finds that there are too many cases in which too little is available in the historical record to help him construct a workable model of how social structures change. The problem with his mathematical modeling had been that it was too static.

Seldon soon becomes interested in a meteorological project under way at the university; the researchers involved are, like himself, having problems modeling chaotic phenomena. When Seldon goes Upperside (outside of the weather-controlled domes of Trantor) to examine how the research is being conducted, he accidentally gets lost and nearly freezes to death after being pursued by a small jet. He is rescued by Dors Venabili, who was able to calculate his position on the surface of a dome from seismographic recordings. The fact that she, a historian, is capable of such reasoning puts her in a different light as well; indeed, she all but admits that she too is a robot at the end of the novel.

Hummin speculates that the Mayor of Wye, a political rival of Cleon's for the Imperial throne, had sent the jet to capture Seldon on the surface. Hummin decides to send Seldon to the second sector of Trantor, Mycogen, where he may be safer and where he can continue his research. As it happens, the Mycogenians cling tightly to a set of traditions about early history and are supposed to have ancient records not available to anyone else, which might aid Seldon in his research on pre-Imperial times.

Seldon explains that as far as simulations and mathematical models are concerned, Galactic society is a kind of limit case: it can be represented by a simulation simpler than itself. Anything larger would require as much complexity in the model as in the object itself. This is what Seldon was able to show in his paper; that one could profitably simulate Galactic society in order to predict future events in a statistical fashion—that is, by stating the probability for alternate sets of events rather than flatly predicting that one set will take place. Seldon also realizes, however, that the construction of such a model would take a billion years. So the quest is still for something simpler yet rich in information.

Asimov deploys some of his best social extrapolation in describing the customs and taboos of the Mycogenians, an ascetic people obsessed with depilatory rituals. Descendants of the Aurorans, they long for a return to the Lost World of the Dawn. They may be intended to suggest a historical parallel with the Jews in exile. On Trantor they have set themselves apart by making a kind of religion of their history and by specializing in the production and development of mycological foods. Mycogenian history contains stories that go back some twenty thousand years and tell of a Renegade humaniform robot who was a traitor to the Auroran cause. As Dors and Seldon discover, there is a real robot at the heart of the Mycogenian Sacratorium, although it has long been inactive. By entering the Sacratorium, Seldon had hoped that he could get the information he needed about early Galactic civilization from the robot's memory, but all he succeeds in doing is violating the most sacred taboos of the Mycogenians. At the moment when Seldon and Dors are faced with death or with being turned over to the Emperor, Hummin—ironically an Honorary Brother of the Mycogenians because he has done them many favors in the past—arrives and persuades the outraged High Elder to release Seldon and Dors into his custody.

The story next leads us to the third sector of Trantor, Dahl, and its infamous shantytown, Billibotton. Asimov's delineation of Dahl is another good piece of social extrapolation. The Dahlites are descendants of Earth's people and maintain themselves in the "heatsinks" of Trantor's energy system. There is a kind of caste system among them that clearly suggests India under British colonialism (just as the Mycogenians, with their rituals, suggest the Jews, and just as the Sacratorium suggests the Wailing Wall, which is part of Solomon's Temple in Jerusalem). Of course, Earth's people have their own legends about the robots.

In Billibotton, Seldon and Dors interview an old woman, Mother Rittah, who tells them that Earth is the original home of humanity—not Aurora, which is an Evil World. With the help of the great hero Ba-Lee and of Da-Nee (a friend of Ba-Lee and an artificial human being who turned against his masters and helped Earth), Earth was able to defeat Aurora and the robots, who were the work of the Evil Worlds. Da-Nee is said never to have died, and is expected to return one day to restore the great old days and remove all cruelty, injustice, and misery.

Before Seldon can make much of this, he is accused of having started a riot in Billibotton and has to escape. He is taken in by Davan, a popular rebel leader. From Davan he learns something of the brutal politics of the Empire, which maintains itself by fostering hatred and suspicion among the sectors. Davan turns Seldon and Dors over to the Mayor of Wye, whose sector is now run by Rashelle, his ambitious daughter. She intends to use Seldon as a spokesman for her political ideas in a bid for power. She wants to let the Empire collapse and simply rule over Trantor; its eight hundred sectors seems world enough for her. She is outmaneuvered by Demerzel, who captures her father and persuades the army that it does not want to be led by a woman.

Seldon finally discovers the double identity of Demerzel and, at the same time, solves the psychohistory problem. Seldon had proved that it was theoretically possible to choose starting conditions from which historical forecasting does not descend into chaos but becomes predictable within limits. What those starting conditions were, however, he did not know. Seldon now realizes that his model must be Trantor itself, with its eight hundred sectors. If he can make psychohistory work first as an approximation of Trantor alone, then the minor effects of the Outer Worlds can be added as later modifications. Seldon believes that with the help of Daneel's vast memory, it might even be possible to work out the fundamentals of psychohistory in his lifetime. Daneel reveals that he has indeed been gently pushing Seldon in that direction all along because of the effect of the Zeroth Law.

The novel ends with Seldon happily in love with Dors Venabili, who may herself be a robot. Also, Daneel reveals that setting up the Foundation on Trantor is just one of his plans. Daneel has two plans for success—two plans to steady the Empire or rebuild it on a new foundation. In order to ensure the success of his plan to save humanity, he has been working on "a separate world in a separate way"—a way that he indicates is in some respects more radical than psychohistory. That world is, of course, the sentient planet Gaia, which we encounter in *Foundation's Edge,* and which eventually supersedes the Seldon Plan.

## *Foundation*

*Foundation* (1951) is now published as the first novel in the so-called Foundation trilogy, but it is somewhat misleading to call it a novel or to say that it is a part of a trilogy of novels. What actually fact happened is this: In the 1940s Asimov wrote a series of eight stories for Campbell's *Astounding* (Campbell's influence, as discussed earlier, is felt in such notions as the Foundation's science of religion) about the fall of the Galactic Empire, loosely inspired by the fall of Rome. He later rearranged the order of these stories to improve their narrative continuity as a novel, and wrote another story to serve as an introduction. This "novel" lacks a central character or hero throughout, though there are heros in each episode, or at least representative types from each social group, such as the Mayors and the Traders.

What lends the book narrative cohesiveness, however, is the much larger story of the stages of the fall of a great Galactic Empire and of Seldon's Plan to rebuild it. When the novel opens, Seldon is an old man in his eighties, and the science of psychohistory has been achieved. It is defined as a "profound statistical science" that deals with the reactions of human conglomerates to fixed social and economic stimuli. Implicit in this definition is the assumption that the human conglomerate being analyzed must be sufficiently large to permit valid statistical treatment. A further assumption is that the human conglomerate in question must be unaware that it is the subject of psychohistorical analysis, to ensure that its reactions are genuine.

These assumptions—especially the latter one—seem to obviate the logical impossibility of knowledge of the future. Put simply, if we could predict future discoveries, they would be present discoveries. These assumptions thus present us with a kind of theoretical history, corresponding to theoretical physics.[2] A more serious problem, though, concerns the notion of fixed stimuli. If science fiction is about the effects of technological and scientific change on society—and this has always been Asimov's definition of it—how can the Foundation trilogy actually be called science fiction? For in it Asimov assumes that in order for psychohistory to operate, there can be no radical technological change.

It may be that the science-fictional aspects of these novels comes not from psychohistory's ability to introduce change, which is minimal, but from its aspect of rational planning for the future, which is the lasting source of its appeal. Asimov brings psychohistory into the scene too late for it to do anything about the fall of the current Empire and the onset of barbarism. But he does use it as a kind of promise to reduce the period of barbarism (the interregnum) from thirty thousand to one thousand years. Psychohistory also promises that in one thousand years a new and greater Empire will be established along more rationalist lines.

In order to accomplish this goal, Seldon, before he dies, manages to convince the authorities on Trantor to establish a Foundation on Terminus, a secluded planet located at the edge of the civilized Galaxy. Thirty thousand physical scientists, with their wives and children, will devote themselves to the preparation of an "Encyclopedia Galactica," a giant summary of all human knowledge. This compilation of knowledge will help shorten the duration of anarchy to a single millennium and act as a scientific refuge. As such, Terminus is supposed to be directly under the Emperor's protection. In addition to the work of the Encyclopedists, as they come to be called, Seldon has also secretly arranged for the establishment of a second Foundation, to be composed of psychohistorians, at an undisclosed place, referred to only as "Star's End." These psychohistorians are to develop covertly mental science and arrange the fulfillment of the Seldon Plan.

The narrative of *Foundation* unfolds as the account of a series of crises in the execution of the Seldon Plan. The first, which occurs fifty years after Seldon's death, involves a tense diplomatic conflict between Terminus and its powerful barbarian neighbor, Anacreon, which wants to annex Terminus. Though it does not possess the metals necessary to maintain a mechanical civilization (it has to trade for them), Terminus does have attractive land on which to set up estates, and this is exactly what the aristocrats of Anacreon want. Terminus is also the only planet in the area which still has atomic power, and this turns out to be crucial to the solution of the crisis. In the middle of the crisis, Seldon himself appears from the Vault in a prerecorded message, telling the leadership of Terminus that the Encyclopedia Foundation is and always had been a fraud. Centered on the past, it could never be a model of scientific discovery. Seldon reveals that by means of the Encyclopedia project, he had kept the scientists busy until it was no longer possible for them to turn back. They now have no choice but to proceed on "the infinitely more important project that was, and is, our real plan."

In keeping with the principles of psychohistory, however, Seldon does not give them any information about this plan. He simply tells them that their history will be a series of crises along one path. He does reassure them, though, that Terminus and its companion Foundation at the other end of the Galaxy are "the seeds of the Renascence" and the future founders of the Second Galactic Empire. As it happens, Terminus must solve its difficulties by itself. This it does by playing the people of Anacreon against their enemies and by rousing those enemies' fears that sole possession of Terminus would make Anacreon too powerful. The other kingdoms force Anacreon to back off from Terminus.

Under the leadership of its first mayor, Salvor Hardin (who appears in two of the stories), the Foundation maintains a precarious independence. But in thirty years' time the Foundation establishes an ascendancy by becoming the religious center of the neighboring kingdoms. It dominates its neighbors by means of atomic energy, out of which it has made a kind of magical religion. Seldon is now the Prophet of the Galactic Spirit, and most of the credulous barbarian masses believe that he appointed the Foundation to carry on his commandments, that there might someday be a return of the Earthly Paradise. Not all believe this, however. Some on Anacreon remember bitterly their humiliation at the hands of the Foundation and plot revenge.

The second crisis occurs when Anacreon recovers an old Imperial battle cruiser and threatens to invade Terminus. The Anacreons attack Terminus, but their own priests are so outraged by this blasphemy against the center of their religion that they lead a successful rebellion. Seldon appears again, this time actually sounding like a prophet. He warns that Spiritual Power cannot prevail against the new forces of Regionalism and Nationalism.

The next two stories take place some fifty and seventy-five years later, respectively. During this time the Foundation's religion-controlled commercial Empire has been expanded by a new social group, the Traders. The Traders are Outlanders, though they receive their educations on Terminus. They are basically irreligious, however, and are only interested in trade itself. Both stories show the rise of a new pragmatism and plutocracy in the political affairs of the Foundation, and an emphasis on enlightened self-interest. In one story the Traders sell technology to a planet on which machines are sacrilegious by appealing to the greed of the rulers; in the other story an attack on Terminus is foiled when Foundation devices on the attacking planet begin to fail. Economic factors force the people to rebel in order to regain their prosperity.

The third crisis occurs when the Korellian Republic, armed with old Empire atomic cruisers, attacks the Foundation. The Korellians, who have a religion based on ancestor worship, are resistant to the influences of the priests of the Foundation. They maintain remnants of various technologies created by the Empire, but will not be able to do so much longer without help from the Empire because of the vast resources required. The technology of the Foundation, on the other hand, has produced small, compact gadgets that are for the most part self-sufficient. As Hober Mallow, the first of the Foundation's Merchant Princes, points out, Seldon crises are not solved by individuals but by historic forces—not by brilliant heroics but by broad sweeps of economics and sociology. Solutions to the various crises must be achieved by the forces that become available at the time.

And so the first part of the trilogy ends: trade without priests and the techniques of economic warfare become the new forces in the Foundation-dominated worlds, but not before Mallow predicts future crises in which money power will be as useless as religion.

## *Foundation and Empire*

At the end of two hundred years of the interregnum, the Foundation is the most powerful state in the Galaxy, except for the remains of the decaying Empire, which still controls three quarters of the population and wealth of the Galaxy. It therefore seems inevitable that the next crisis facing the Foundation will be a battle with the Empire. The second book of the Foundation trilogy, *Foundation and Empire* (1952), in divided into two parts.

The first and shortest part is about a general named Bel Riose who attempts to find the Magicians on Terminus and defeat them, thereby winning military glory. The second and longer part concerns the activities of a mutant, the Mule, who is not predicted by Seldon's Plan and therefore represents the greater threat.

The story of Bel Riose, an ambitious and capable young general of the decaying Empire, is one in which the individual, despite his considerable energy and acumen, is done in by the dead hand of historical necessity. The Merchant Princes who are the Foundation's leaders have no idea how to stop Riose, but they send a Trader, Lathan Devers, to be captured by Riose and to report on the general's activities. Before Riose can accomplish his goal, however, the Emperor becomes suspicious of Riose's request for more ships to attack the Foundation, recalls him, and has him executed for being a threat to his power.

On first hearing of Seldon's theories from an old patrician (Ducem Barr, who is something of an authority on the Foundation), Riose had proclaimed that he was not "a silly robot following a predetermined course into destruction." Riose is by no means a silly figure, but nonetheless he remains clasped tightly in the controlling hand of psychohistorical forces.

Those forces are analyzed very much after the fact by Barr, and in retrospect what happened to Riose seems to have been inevitable. The social background of the Empire, which Seldon would have understood, makes wars of conquest impossible for it. Under weak Emperors it is torn apart by generals competing for the throne. Under strong Emperors it is paralyzed and cannot grow because such Emperors fear their generals. Events of the past two centuries had shown that three-fourths of the Emperors were rebel generals before becoming Emperor. Only the combination of a strong Emperor and a strong general—a combination not allowed by the logic of the current social situation—could harm the Foundation, for a strong Emperor cannot be dethroned easily, and a strong general is forced to turn outward, past the frontiers. Barr predicts that the Empire can never threaten the Foundation again, and the Seldon Plan seems unshakably on course.

But Asimov's editor, Campbell, urged him to write a story in which the Seldon Plan is upset. Asimov came up with a novella, "The Mule," which appeared in the December 1945 issue of *Astounding*. The story takes place 105 years after the execution of Riose and the last Seldon crisis. Many of the Traders (traditionally hostile to the Foundation) believe that another crisis is pending, because in their eyes every vice of the Empire has been repeated by the Foundation, including inertia of the ruling classes (the merchant princes), despotism, and maldistribution of wealth. The Traders on some of the smaller planets actually seek to provoke a crisis, or at least to take advantage of one, in order to gain a greater degree of economic freedom. To one of these planets, Haven, have come rumors of a strange, irresistible man, known as the Mule, who has begun to conquer worlds. Bayta Darell and her husband, Toran, leave Haven for Kalgan, a world recently defeated by the Mule, to investigate.

While on Kalgan the two take into their protection the Mule's Fool, Magnifico, who has escaped his cruel master. The Mule uses this "kidnapping" of his Fool as an excuse to attack the Foundation. When Seldon finally does appear in a simulacrum from the Vault during this fifth crisis (it is revealed that he had appeared at the proper time for the last two as well, but was ignored), he speaks of a "logical civil war forced upon the Foundation." It is evident that he has in mind the wrong (although a related) crisis, and as a result the science of psychohistory itself seems to be in crisis.

Nothing can stop the Mule, who has gained a reputation as a mutant superman. He wins battle after battle, conquering even Terminus. Some, such as Captain Han Pritcher of the Foundation Fleet, are converted to the idea that the Mule is the fulfillment of Seldon's dream of Galactic unification seven hundred years before he had hoped to see it. But others know that the realization of Seldon's dream does not depend on a single individual, however powerful.

Bayta, Toran and Ebling Mis, a Foundation scientist who is trying to rebuild the science of psychohistory, escape to Haven with Magnifico. When Haven too comes under attack, the four are sent to Trantor so that Mis can use the great Imperial University Library to research information about the location of the Second Foundation. This information might aid them in defeating the Mule.

The old Imperial capitol, now called Neotrantor, itself is in ruins, having been sacked by a rebellious general. The four are captured by the heir to the throne, Dagobert IX, who is killed soon after when Magnifico plays his Visi-Sonor at a high amplitude. The captives escape to the Library, where an agricultural community has developed. Mis begins searching the records, but he soon grows ill, the victim of a kind of despair. Searching for the flaw in Seldon's Plan, Mis tells Bayta that any major change in the technology of the Galaxy would cause social changes that would render Seldon's original equations obsolete. But since this has not happened, it must be the second assumption of psychohistory that has been affected. Human reactions to stimuli have not remained constant. Some factor must be twisting and distorting the emotional responses of human beings, or Seldon could not have failed.

On the verge of death and about to reveal the location of the Second Foundation (in whose mental powers, he believes, Seldon had indeed planned for such an eventuality as the Mule), Mis is shot and killed by Bayta, who now realizes that Magnifico is the Mule. The Mule is a telepath who exhibits mental dominance, but in the case of Bayta his own emotions had played him false. He had not juggled her emotions to convert her to his cause, as he had done with Han Pritcher and countless others, because she had given him her sympathy freely.

*Foundation and Empire* ends with the Mule's temporary defeat, but he remains determined to locate and destroy the Second Foundation. In the reading Bayta gives to events, the Foundation itself was only a minor victory for the Mule, since it was not designed to stop his kind of crisis. With some vehemence she predicts that the Second Foundation, now alerted to his presence, will be ready for him and will defeat him; he will be "just another strutting conqueror, flashing quickly and meanly across the bloody face of history." At any rate, the Mule knows that he will never establish a dynasty, for like his namesake, the Mule is sterile.

## *Second Foundation*

With the concluding novel of the trilogy, Asimov returns to a narrative pattern he knows well: the mystery. *Second Foundation* (1953) is divided into two parts, each taking the form of a search for the Second Foundation. The first, "Search by the Mule," takes place some five years after the end of *Foundation and Empire*. In the meantime, the Mule has consolidated his empire into a tightly controlled Union of Worlds. The Foundation leaders he had found useless are now dead, and those he had found useful (such as Han Pritcher, now a general) are now converted to his cause. The Mule rules his empire from the planet Kalgan, where he has enlisted the services of one of its free, expansive souls who thrive on war and adventure, Bail Channis. The Mule leaves Channis unconverted in the hope that he can detect any attempt by the Second Foundation to tamper with Channis. Several of the Mule's key men have been tampered with: their loyalty has been left intact, but their initiative and ingenuity have been rubbed out. Unbeknownst to the Mule, however, Channis is actually an agent of the Second Foundation.

Pritcher had been searching unsuccessfully for the Second Foundation for the past five years. Now he is sent out again with the capable Channis. For the first time in the trilogy, we encounter Second Foundation psychologists who are monitoring the situation, including the First Speaker himself, though we are kept from knowing where Star's End is until the end of the second part of the book. Channis decides that Star's End must be the planet Tazenda, which controls its neighboring planet, Rossem, with no obvious signs of political domination. Yet the Elders of Rossem hold Tazenda in terror. This seems to point to the evidence of mental science for which the Mule has been searching.

Not long after Pritcher and Channis land on Rossem, however, we are led astray by a false solution to the mystery. After some inquiries, Pritcher accuses Channis of treason against the Mule, because he found the location of the Second Foundation too easily. But then the Mule arrives, having used a "hypertracer" to follow their ship (Asimov allows some technological innovation under the Mule's reign, especially in the area of interstellar travel). The Mule reveals that he has used Channis to lead him to the Second Foundation and that he has already destroyed Tazenda. Under the Mule's mental pressure, Channis admits what he has been prepared by the Second Foundation to believe: that Rossem, not Tazenda, is the location of the Second Foundation.

The Mule's conversations with Channis present a new interpretation of the Seldon Plan. Channis argues that the laws of psychohistory are not absolute, but relative. Seldon had created not a finished product in psychohistory but an "evolving mechanism," and the Second Foundation is the instrument of its evolution. The Mule remains unimpressed with the grandeur of the Seldon Plan. He continues to destroy Channis's will to resist until the First Speaker, the leading psychologist of the Second Foundation, arrives and reveals that Channis had been convinced that Rossem was the location, but it was not. It had all been a ploy to lure the Mule to Rossem so that Foundation psychologists could start a rebellion on Kalgan in his absence. The Mule's empire is done.

In the despair of the moment, while the defenses of the Mule's mind are lowered, the First Speaker reconstructs the Mule's memory so that he does not remember their encounter. The Mule retains his mental powers, but his motivations are now entirely different. The notion of a Second Foundation is no longer with him, and he is a man of peace. In a last interlude, the "emotional surgery" that adjusted Channis's mind is undone, and his original mind, which knows the real location of the Second Foundation, is restored to him. It is made clear that the Seldon Plan will go on after the death of the Mule but that it cannot work on its own anymore. It will need adjustments and alterations.

On the basis of a bare summary of the plot, it may be difficult to understand the excitement and appeal these early stories held for readers of Campbell's *Astounding,* where they first appeared—yet they certainly command readerly involvement. The first part of *Second Foundation* is a minor masterpiece of paranoid knowledge. The Mule himself is described by the Second Foundation not only as a megalomaniac (which they were prepared to deal with) but also as an "intensely psychopathic paranoid," obsessed with finding out which of the minds under his control have been tampered with. This required Asimov to incorporate the ruse of having Channis submit to "emotional surgery" in order to convince the Mule that he is one of the Unconverted—someone whom the Mule can watch for signs of interference. In fact we are never sure in the story, until near the end, just who is under whose mental influence.

Indeed, it is strongly suggested that Pritcher unbeknownst even to himself, may be an agent of the Second Foundation. The fear that Pritcher feels in examining his own mind for traces of mental influence is effectively dramatized and pushes at the limits of what reason can know. The story is cleverly designed to make the reader paranoid; it becomes a kind of game in which the reader is led to form hypotheses about who is a Second Foundation agent. Like the Mule, the reader is caught up in a double game, suspecting everyone but the reasonable Channis. It is, of course, an irony of the story that the Mule's powers are limited to those of emotional adjustment. He cannot adjust reason, which remains inviolate in the Asimovian universe.

Not all Asimovian narrative has this paranoid intensity to it, but the later Foundation novels continue in the same vein. Because Asimov is not limited in terms of the length of these novels, he is able to add more and more levels of paranoid knowledge to the story. The reader wonders what is the mysterious third force manipulating both the First and the Second Foundations, and speculates, along with the characters, that it may be a planet of Anti-Mules (to be discussed). Paranoia is the vehicle for the reader's involvement in "Seldon's cosmic chess game." More than anything else, it holds the series together.

The second part of the novel, "Search by the Foundation," takes place about seventy years later. The old Empire based on Trantor is completely dead, as is the Mule, but the period of the Mule's enlightened despotism has put an end to the era of the warlords who preceded him. As for the Foundation, it has risen again. The planet Terminus houses the center of a commercial federation almost a great and rich as it was before the conquest, and even more peaceful and civilized. There are no longer dissident worlds of independent Traders, and no apparent danger to the Seldon Plan—unless it is true, as some now claim, that the Second Foundation itself represents a danger.

Science and technological innovation have begun to flourish again on Terminus, and certain scientists have made breakthroughs in electroencephalography, a new science that has enabled them to analyze brain-wave patterns. What they have discovered is disturbing: some of the highest political and cultural leaders of Terminus manifest a "Tamper plateau" and are probably being manipulated by the Second Foundation. The scientists, horrified by the idea that their own minds might be controlled, form a conspiracy to defeat the Second Foundation by developing (among other things) a Mental Static device that can counter the effects of emotional manipulation.

The general population of Terminus, while complacent about the inevitable success of the Seldon Plan, regards the Second Foundation with distinct ambivalence. As the "true" heirs and guardians of the Seldon Plan, they hate and envy the supposed superiority of the Second Foundation, yet they rely on it implicitly for protection.

All this points to another crisis in the Seldon Plan. Because the First Foundation now knows of the existence of the Second Foundation in detail rather than through an ancient and vague statement of Seldon's, it has lost initiative and become a decadent and hedonistic culture. Nevertheless, according to the mathematics of psychohistory, and in particular to Korillov's Theorem, knowledge of the Foundation's guardianship and its control will arouse hostility among a few individuals, who may try to become psychologists. So the problem has two aspects: how to get the Plan back on course by making the Foundation civilization self-propelled again, and how to deal with those hostile individuals—something the Plan was never intended to address.

In order to get at the people problem, the Second Foundation sends a man named Pelleas Anthor to Terminus as its agent. An expert in encephalography, he is to attempt to control the conspirators, who are nominally led by Dr. Toran Darell. Unbeknownst to us, the Second Foundation also controls Arkady, Darell's fourteen-year-old daughter, who was tampered with as an infant. She becomes the main tool in convincing her father that Anthor is a Second Foundation agent and that the Second Foundation is located on Terminus (a false solution to the mystery of its whereabouts).

The conspirators, determined to locate the Second Foundation, send Homir Munn, a librarian and expert on the Mule, to Kalgan. His mission is to find out what he can from the library in the Mule's old palace. The current Lord of Kalgan, Stettin, styles himself First Citizen of the Galaxy, in imitation of the Mule's only title; he likes to entertain the idea that he too can be a conqueror. The romantic young Arkady (who is Bayta Darell's granddaughter) stows away on this trip. She proves helpful on Kalgan by persuading Lord Stettin's mistress, Lady Callia (another Second Foundation agent) that Munn intends to prove that the Second Foundation does not exist and that Lord Stettin is destined to unite the Galaxy.

Stettin permits Munn's research in the old palace but also decides he wants to marry Arkady. Callia helps Arkady escape. She is nearly captured at the spaceport on Kalgan but is saved by an elderly couple, Preem Palver and his wife, who are trading representatives of their farm cooperative on Trantor. (The Yiddish-inflected English of the two—especially of the wife—is a source of comic relief.) They take Arkady back to Trantor. Meanwhile, Stettin attacks the Foundation and appears to be winning, but in a final battle his fleet is wiped out. It appears that Stettin is defeated more by the myth of the infallibility of Seldon's Plan than by any fault in his battle plan. His men are fundamentally reluctant to attack because they believe that the Second Foundation will inevitably intervene at the last moment.

The defeat of Stettin shows the Foundation that it can beat a physical enemy and wipe out the damage done to its self-esteem and self-assuredness by the Mule. Once this has been accomplished and the civilization of the Foundation has been set back on course, the Second Foundation can appear to destroy itself. This is accomplished through individuals. Arkady sends a cryptic message from Trantor telling her father that "a circle has no end." From this he deduces that the Second Foundation is on Terminus itself. Toran Darell then uses his Mental Static device on Anthor. Anthor "admits" that the Kalganian war was just a distraction, just as Toran had suspected, and that there are others like him operating on Terminus, which is the real home of the Second Foundation. Fifty men and women of the Second Foundation are sacrificed, but the Seldon Plan has been restored, for the Foundation now believes that it has wiped them all out. Furthermore, the science of electroencephalography, which had threatened their power, will no longer have any impetus, since the threat of mental dominance by the Second Foundation has been removed. However, the Second Foundation is actually located on Trantor, where its psychologists appear to be simple farmers. The First Speaker, Preem Palver, finally clarifies Seldon's obscure remark about the Second Foundation being located at "the opposite end of the Galaxy." Our Galaxy is a double spiral. From its periphery, the opposite end of a spiral is its center, Trantor (which, moreover, was the socially opposite end of the Galaxy from Terminus in Seldon's time).

## *Foundation's Edge*

*Foundation's Edge* (1982) takes place one hundred and twenty years later, or five hundred years into the Seldon Plan. It is the year 498 F.E., and the Foundation has experienced nearly two centuries of peace. Just as Seldon had predicted, it has become a Federation of planets, halfway to an Empire. The first two centuries had been the Golden Age and Heroic Era of the Foundation, but there have been no heroes or even figures of romance since the Kalganian war. Terminus is now run by tough-minded pragmatists such as Mayor Harla Branno. As the novel opens, she has just seen the Foundation through another crisis that could have led to civil war. Some wanted to locate the capital in the prestige-filled interior of the Galaxy because of its aura of Imperial power. But with the help of Seldon's simulacrum, Branno had won out. The capital will be on Terminus, and Branno has announced that she will henceforth tolerate no public displays of doubt or criticism concerning the Seldon Plan.

This stance brings her into conflict with one of her own Councilmen, Golan Trevize, an unusually self-assured and combative fellow who is the hero of this novel (and of the last novel of the series, *Foundation and Earth*). Trevize, who has great powers of intuition and logic, believes that the Second Foundation was never destroyed by the First, as commonly believed. To his mind, there is something too perfect about the operation of the Plan for it not to be guided by some other agency. When he confides his theories to his fellow Councilman, Munn Li Compor, Compor betrays him to Branno, ostensibly out of patriotic motives. Trevize is sent into exile without a trial.

Mayor Branno, who also suspects that the Second Foundation may still exist, decides to use Trevize as a "lightning rod" to attract its attention. At her command, Trevize embarks on an open-ended quest for Earth (where he believes the Second Foundation is located) with Janov Pelorat, who is to provide a cover and mask for the mission. Pelorat is a professor of history obsessed with myths and legends of isolated worlds and particularly desirous of finding the Earth, "the incredible prize."

To help them on their search for Earth, the two are equipped with one of the Foundation's latest technological marvels, a gravitic (antigravity) ship, which contains a computer that can be directed by thought. Asimov revels in the details of how the ship negotiates the Jump through hyperspace and in the strange sensations that human-computer interface brings. The Foundation had always led the Galaxy in the development of miniaturization, but these technological advances had not affected the Seldon Plan. As Branno knows, however, in the past century the Foundation had made rapid progress in the fields of gravitics and electroencephalography (mental shielding). As a science, electroencephalography had seemingly been made sterile at the end of *Second Foundation,* but Branno reveals that research has continued in secret. She believes that the Seldon Plan and "this semimythical science of psychohistory," cannot serve the Foundation much longer. They are products of a bygone time and soon will be obsolete. Furthermore, with the advent of mental shielding, the Second Foundation—if its exists—will not be able to control them much longer either. Cynically, she hopes that the Second Foundation does exist, so that she can defeat it and establish an ostentatious imperial empire in the last days of her power.

Branno decides to send an apparently unwilling Compor to follow Trevize in his wanderings. Actually, this is just what Compor wants, for he is an agent of the Second Foundation, an Observer with somewhat lesser mental powers than the psychohistorians on Trantor, to whom he reports.

The novel paints a not-very-pretty picture of life in a mentalic society, in which no one can hide his or her true purposes very effectively from others. Nonetheless, vicious political rivalry often occurs, especially concerning the appointment of a new First Speaker. Trevize has his counterpart in the keen-minded Speaker Stor Gendibal, who is the apparent heir to the position. Like Trevize, though, Gendibal has some radical ideas about the status of the Seldon Plan. His argument is that it is working too perfectly, that its flaw is its flawlessness. Gendibal comes up with a truly paranoid idea about why things have been going so smoothly since the defeat of the Mule: a third party, a "mystery organization" with even greater mental powers than those of the Second Foundation, must be manipulating events.

Following a suggestion of Quindor Shandess, the current First Speaker, Gendibal tentatively calls this organization the Anti-Mules and postulates that they are operating from a hidden planet. He even speculates that Branno acted under compulsion from agents of the Anti-Mules when she exiled Trevize, whom he believes has been recruited by them to spearhead the destruction of the Second Foundation. Gendibal's political rivals, in particular a woman named Dolora Delarmi, try to discredit Gendibal's theories.

One thing that had convinced Gendibal of tampering is that all references to Earth in the library have been eradicated. But this is not enough to convince his enemies. He undergoes a trial by mental probing, but wins out because he finally presents one piece of irrefutable evidence that a mind has been tampered with by powers greater than those known to the Second Foundation.

Previously an attempt had been made on Gendibal's life by a group of

Hamish farmers, who usually hold the "scowlers" of the library in a kind of uneasy reverence. Gendibal had been saved by a young peasant girl, Sura Novi, who now wants to accompany him and be a scholar herself. On examining her mind, Gendibal had discovered that it had been delicately tampered with. On examination, the other Speakers can clearly see the truth of his assertion that some tampering has been done.

Gendibal is sent out to follow Trevize; he is disguised as a Hamish Trader, and Novi poses as his wife. She is to act as an early-warning system in which Gendibal can detect the first symptomatic presence of mentalism by the Anti-Mules. What he does not know is that Novi is in fact an agent of the Anti-Mules, who inhabit a sentient planet called Gaia.

Trevize and Pelorat are led to Gaia by the surviving myths and legends of Earth. Initially the search takes them away from Trantor to the Sayshell sector, which has maintained its independence at the Foundation's edge (hence the title). Pelorat and Trevize discover that according to the myths of this planet, it has been protected by Gaia since before the time of Hari Seldon. Asimov makes all the myths and legends of this world reflect (with small distortions) the story line of the robot novels and the two waves of colonization, one aided by robots (i.e., that of Aurora and the Outer Worlds) and one not (i.e., that carried out by the Settlers of the later robot novels). In doing so he weaves a science-fiction universe that encompasses all his novels in terms of history, science, and myth.

Gaia is not Earth, though it is indeed the planet of the Mule, a criminal who escaped from Gaia. It represents the second alternative path for mankind's survival mentioned by R. Daneel Olivaw at the end of *Prelude to Foundation*. Apparently the robots had been able to transfer their capacity for mental telepathy—and also the Three Laws of Robotics—to a group of humans who first colonized Gaia over twenty thousand years ago. Over the centuries the planet has grown into a single sentient world in rational ecological balance, from the stones in the mountains to its human inhabitants. Trevize and Pelorat first encounter Bliss, a young woman, and Dom, who seems to be the planet's spokesman. Dom tells them a fable about the creation of the time line they all now inhabit (which is basically the plot of *The End of Eternity;* see chapter 1). He even suggests that the Eternals may have been robots working to create an all-human Galaxy for mankind's survival. What is most important, however, is that Trevize, because of his uncanny intuitive ability to make the right choice, has been guided to Gaia to solve the upcoming crisis between the First and Second Foundations.

It is true that Gaia has been manipulating events, bringing representatives from both Foundations to the edge of the Galaxy, but because of the

Three Laws of Robotics it cannot directly interfere. A kind of stalemate is reached; Gaia offers a solution, but it has to be freely chosen. As Novi explains to Gendibal, the Second Empire, structured in the fashion of Terminus, would be militaristic and would eventually be destroyed by strife. The Second Empire, modeled on Trantor, would be paternalistic, established by calculation, and a perpetual living death—a hell of individual egos struggling for dominance. What Gaia offers is life in the form of Galaxia, a living, remembering Galaxy—"a way of life fundamentally different from all that has gone before and repeating none of the old mistakes."

Not surprisingly, Trevize chooses Galaxia. Branno, who had followed Trevize because she suspected that Compor was a double agent, has her mind adjusted so that she forgets about the development of a mentalic field. She goes back to Terminus thinking that she has arranged a favorable commercial treaty with Sayshell. The Speaker from the Second Foundation, Stor Gendibal, goes back to Trantor convinced that he has arranged it. Novi returns with him to assure that the changes that will bring about Galaxia are initiated. And neither Foundation is aware that Gaia exists.

At the end of the novel everyone is apparently satisfied, except for Trevize, who in true Asimovian manner does not willingly accept ignorance. In particular, he wants to know what happened to the robots, and why the Earth remains hidden. He even accuses Bliss of being a "robot supervisor" of the planet Gaia, and she does not deny it. Trevize does not fit in the world of Gaia. He will soon embark on another quest for knowledge.

## *Foundation and Earth*

*Foundation and Earth* (1987) opens soon after the end of *Foundation's Edge*. Trevize wants to know the answer to two mysteries: why did he choose Galaxia, "this dreadful fate for humanity," over the individuality of isolated persons and worlds, and why is there no information about the Earth anywhere, not even on Gaia? Trevize leaves Gaia on a quest to discover the answer to these questions, accompanied by Bliss and Pelorat, a recent convert to the joys of merging with Gaia. Trevize remains stubbornly aloof from Bliss, however, and there is a running debate throughout the book between Trevize, who extols the value of individuality, opposition, and rebellion, and Bliss and Pelorat, who have chosen the comfortable and secure tameness of Gaia, where every consciousness is subtly adjusted to the benefit of the superorganism. To Bliss and Pelorat, Gaia may seem like "the planetary version of a comfortable house," but to Trevize it is a world of unbearable sameness in which no individuals, whether saints or sinners, stand out from the norm.

Furthermore, progress and development have been slowed, if not stopped altogether, on Gaia. Trevize thinks of Gaia as a "Galactic kraken" spreading its tentacles of consciousness throughout the Galaxy, but as a mythologic power it lacks the ability to induce novelty and change.

Nor does the Seldon Plan fare very much better, in his critical view. Trevize now equates the Plan with superstition because it seems to direct actions in the absence of knowledge. The Foundation believes in the Seldon Plan, although no one in it can understand the Plan, interpret its details, or use it to make predictions. Trevize believes that he has found a major flaw in the Seldon Plan—some hidden or unacknowledged third assumption beside the initial two, which require people to be both numerous and unaware. What this third assumption is he does not yet know, though he knows that the Seldon Plan has been derailed by Galaxia, which is "utterly different" from anything in history. We can probably guess, however, that it is in some way related to the central values of science-fiction narrative—the introduction of the novum, or technological change, that is irreversible.[3] In this sense, Trevize is a spokesman for the (predominantly male) science-fiction reader and perhaps for Asimov himself, who seems to be searching in this novel for an understanding of difference, both sexual and political.

With this in mind, it must be said that the other side of the argument for Galaxia is well presented by Bliss and Pelorat, at least insofar as they understand its purpose (and a more rational basis is given for Galaxia's existence at the end). We feel that Bliss is right in her assertion that the world of Isolates, as she calls it, has always been one of misery and bloodshed—a Galaxy of Anarchy. And we are deeply drawn to the pleasures of a planet on which each inhabitant may share the pleasures of the others. Yet we are kept not entirely comfortable with this alternative either, which would be a Galaxy in which an ultimate Unity reigns. Trevize is not prepared to say that total Unification is good because total Isolation is bad (on each one of the isolated worlds they visit, something malignant or dangerous to outsiders happens)—and neither are we, at least not until we have all the available information.

In order to get at this information, the three visit a series of planets, following the legends of Earth as they grow less and less distorted, until they arrive at Earth, where the final secrets are revealed. The first planet they visit is Comporellon, or "Benbally World," whose legends hold that it was the first planet colonized by the second wave of Settlers from Earth, and that Earth is "nearby." Comporellon is an Associated Power not directly under

Foundation authority, and jealous of its power. It is a puritanical, sexually repressed society with rigidly applied laws, vaguely reminiscent of Soviet Russia. Mitza Lizalor, Minister of Transportation, wants to seize the Foundation's marvelous gravitic ship, and has the three arrested on what amounts to a morals charge (throughout the trip, Bliss serves Pelorat's sexual needs). Mitza herself is aroused by Trevize, however, and after a night of sexual sporting with him, she agrees to let the travelers go, not least because she is disturbed at their proclaimed destination. No one who has sought Earth—the "Oldest one," the planet punished and made radioactive because it used robots—has ever returned. What is more, the entire history of the Spacer/Settler colonization of the Galaxy is recounted to Trevize and Pelorat by Dr. Vasil Deniador, a Comporellian Skeptic, who tells them that he does not know the location of the Earth and that it is useless to look for it. Such a lack of interest on the part of a scientist fuels their suspicion that Earth may be powerful enough to prevent anyone from finding it.

On leaving Comporellon, the three make the Jump through hyperspace and find what turns out to be the planet Aurora, greatest of the Spacer worlds. In the past twenty thousand years it has fallen into decay—"unterraformed" itself to the extent that its only current inhabitants are a gang of wild dogs. Next they visit Solaria, where the secret of what happened to the Solarians is revealed: they have gone underground. They are met by a latter-day Solarian, Sarton Bander, who explains that the Solarians have transformed themselves genetically into hermaphrodites, thereby pushing their goal of absolute individual freedom close to its ideal limits. They have also developed new organs, transducer lobes located behind the ears, which enable them to mentally transform the planet's thermal radiation in order to run their robots and perform feats of telekinesis. The Solarians regard themselves as whole human beings and call others half-human. Furthermore, they regard their new organs to be what distinguishes Solarians from everyone else. They have refused to compete in the colonization of the Galaxy. They believe that the Swarmers (colonizers) will eventually kill each other off, and await the day when they, the Solarians—whole, solitary, and liberated—will have the Galaxy to themselves.

Though arrogant, Bander at first seems very hospitable toward the three travelers, whom he regards as creatures in the same class as the thousands of robots that manage his estate. He even shows them his ancestral death chambers, although such acts of showing and seeing based on personal presence are considered shameful by other Solarians. He tells them that he is going to kill them, but before he can do so, Bliss uses her mental powers to block his attempt, and he dies. The three escape to the surface, but not before Bliss detects the presence of a Solarian child, Fallom, whom they take with them after destroying its robot guardian. Bliss takes the child, who has remarkable learning powers, under her maternal wing. Eventually the three "decide" to consider the child a female.

The horrors of Solaria behind them, the four proceed to the planet Melpomenia, another decaying Spacer world. There they discover a Hall of Worlds, which lists the coordinates of the fifty Spacer worlds. Though the planet is uninhabited, they are attacked by a mosslike substance that grows on their space suits. By feeding the appropriate coordinates into the computer, they are able to locate the planet Alpha, or New Earth, and realize that they are very close to the end of their search. On Alpha, which is mainly a water world terraformed into one island, they discover a society that is advanced in biotechnology and can also control the weather (although it does not have advanced electronics). According to local legend, Alpha was the planet designated by the Trantor of Imperial times as a replacement for the old radioactive Earth, which was ultimately evacuated. It was later abandoned by Trantor in a time of economic difficulty. The inhabitants had since evolved toward becoming amphibians (they plan to develop gills as well as lungs) so that they can live in the oceans.

On the surface, Alpha seems friendly, a kind of tropical paradise, but actually the Alphans are bent on preserving their isolation. Through a sexual encounter with a native girl, Hiroko, Trevize is infected with a inactive but fatal virus that is to be activated later. When Fallom performs beautifully on a flute at a music festival, however, a moved Hiroko confesses that the infection is part of a plot to kill Trevize. The four travelers escape from Alpha. With the information they have accumulated on Alpha and the other planets they have visited, they can now locate Earth, which is indeed radioactive and uninhabited. Trevize soon deduces that the secret they have been searching for lies on Earth's moon, and Bliss detects "something new" inhibiting it—an intelligence that is neither human nor robotic.

That intelligence—one unlike any that has existed before—resides within R. Daneel Olivaw, who lives with other robots inside a vast and complex hollow mountain. Having lived and accumulated memories for twenty thousand years, Daneel's mind is certainly advanced beyond that of any other robot that ever existed. It cannot be said to be simply robotic, but neither can it be considered human.

In the last chapter of *Foundation and Earth,* Asimov seems to be signaling the reader about important science-fictional changes (something new, or the novum) in his imaginative universe. For the encounter with Daneel's new and different mind provokes Trevize into thinking something new—a third basic law or axiom of psychohistory that is more fundamental than the other two—just as Daneel and his colleague Giskard worked out the the Zeroth Law of Robotics.

Daneel and his fellow robots—distributed over the Galaxy in an effort to influence a person here, a person there—have been active in shaping the history and survival of mankind over the past twenty thousand years (since the end of *Robots and Empire*). They have been limited in what they could do by the existence of the Laws of Robotics, however. They had done their best to salvage Earth after it began to turn radioactive. At one time Daneel had started the recycling of Earth's soil (a tie-in with *Pebble in the Sky*) and, much later, the terraforming of Alpha. In neither case had he been truly successful. The robots had found it difficult to deal with humanity in concrete terms, but with the discovery of the Zeroth Law they began to think of humanity in the abstract. They had attempted to resolve this contradiction by converting humanity into a single superorganism: Gaia.

Daneel had engineered the founding of Gaia and inculcated the humans there with the Three Laws of Robotics so that they would value the superorganism over the individual. Daneel retains his own freedom of action, but the inhabitants of Gaìa cannot know about it. This explains the necessity for a hidden Earth; indeed, Daneel's robots had systematically removed all references to Earth from recorded sources.

Gaia itself, however, has not been entirely successful. In particular, the start-up time for the project had taken much longer than originally anticipated. Only in the past century had Gaia become fully established and ready to move down what may prove to be a long, long road to Galaxia. Five centuries ago, when it had seemed that Daneel would never overcome all the obstacles to establishing Gaia, he had turned to "the second-best" approach: helping to develop psychohistory (a tie-in with *Prelude to Foundation*). Within the current narrative's time frame, Daneel has manipulated the minds of most of the characters (through Bliss), strengthening impulses already present, in order to bring them to his base on the moon, where they must aid him in a problem that has become desperate: he is dying.

That is, Daneel's positronic brain, which has been rebuilt five times, is reaching the limits of its capacity. He must transfer his knowledge to a brain that operates without the Three Laws of Robotics if Galaxia is to be successful. Trevize refuses to let it be his brain on the grounds that he will lose his individuality, Pelorat is not a candidate for the knowledge transfer because he will not live long enough, and Daneel does not want to merge with Gaia through Bliss. That leaves Fallom, the Spacer child, who has the required life span and mental capacity. Hints in the narrative indicate that Daneel may have been manipulating events all along to bring the child to him.

Trevize now discovers why he chose Galaxia over Seldon's Second Empire: there is a flaw in the Seldon Plan; it does not allow for "something new" to happen (as mentioned earlier, the Plan did not allow for any rapid technological change). What Trevize has discovered, however, is that the Plan also does not allow for "something new" in the form of an intelligence widely different in nature—specifically, an alien intelligence whose behavior could not be described accurately by the mathematics of psychohistory.

It emerges that Galaxia is the best defense against an alien invasion of our Galaxy, for it cannot be turned against itself (to a large extent, human history has been humans fighting humans) and could meet invaders with maximum power. Trevize now understands that in only a few more centuries, human civilization will be safe. This ending is worthy of the best classic science fiction of the Golden Age, which Asimov helped to shape. It has resonances that go all the way back to *The End of Eternity,* in which an all-human galaxy was established. But it does not entirely remain within those aesthetic norms. For if Trevize represents the typical heroic male intellectual in science fiction, who seeks novelty and change—and I think it is fair to say that he does—then he will have to think through the difference represented by Fallom who, Asimov suggests, may be the alien among us. Fallom's sexual ambiguousness had made Trevize, the typical male science-fiction hero, uneasy all along. Perhaps Fallom signals the presence of something not entirely rational in the Asimovian universe. At any rate, the fate and destiny of the Galaxy and of humankind now depend on this strange new creature, "hermaphroditic, transductive, different," that will be even stranger after it receives Daneel's perfect memories. It would seem that science fiction in the Asimovian universe has departed considerably from the norms established by Campbell during the Golden Age.

## *Chapter Seven*

# Critical Summary

### Asimov's Other Fiction

In addition to his novels, Asimov has written hundreds of short stories, some of which have been studied by Joseph Patrouch.[1] Those stories which are tied into Asimov's larger imaginative universe—the focus of this study—have already been discussed (see chapter 2), and those which played a significant role in the development of his career (such as "Nightfall") have been mentioned (see chapter 1). What remains to be provided is an account of his other major attempts at the science-fiction novel that are not connected (at least, not yet) with his larger imaginative universe.

Foremost among these is *The Gods Themselves* (1972) which won both the Hugo and Nebula awards in 1973 for best science-fiction novel. The book is based on the hard science of nuclear physics, from which it extrapolates. Although the science in it may seem esoteric to the average reader, Asimov presents his ideas in his typically clear manner.

Although Asimov has always maintained that he long ago gave up any thought of writing anything poetic or symbolic or experimental, this novel may be the one exception. Apparently it was written as a response to the challenge of writing science fiction in the 1970s, which had largely moved beyond him, owing to the stylistic experimentation of the New Wave. James Gunn has pointed out the few stylistic innovations that Asimov allows, including chapters out of sequence and chapters bearing alphabetic signs to indicate which point of view is being followed. In Gunn's opinion, the most important thing about the book was that it constituted an important statement by Asimov: that science could still be the distinguishing characteristic of science fiction and that the older traditions could be built upon rather than discarded.[2] This concept raises the issues of Asimov's willingness to change and his perceived status, among some, as a has-been (or "old dinosaur," as Brian Aldiss has put it) within the science-fiction community. I will take up these issues later.

All else aside, there is no question that *The Gods Themselves,* a sterling example of hard-core science fiction, is at the same time critical of the scientific establishment—although it never expresses a loss of faith in its rationality. It also contains some of the most convincing alien intelligences ever devised—perhaps Asimov's response to the fact that his all-human Galaxy had prevented him from confronting Otherness. The book is divided into three parts, and the central part is taken up by the aliens, who of course have their own science. The story opens in the early twenty-first century. The aliens inhabit a parallel Universe in which the laws of nuclear physics, and therefore the basic fabric of reality, are different. In particular, nuclear force is much stronger in their Universe, so that nuclear fusion is more likely to occur than fission, the likely occurrence in our Universe. Because the aliens feed on energy and their sun is burning out, they contact our Universe in order to arrange a transfer of energy. (Energy is needed for their sexual reproduction, a process in which a Rational and a Parental are allowed to merge by an Emotional, who supplies the energy to transfer a seed from the Rational to the Parental and thereby to form a new triad.) The end products of the aliens' evolution, the Hard Ones, design a technology of energy transfer, embodied in an instrument called an Electron Pump. Their superior intelligence has made possible its many benefits, which include a copious and clean energy source that has transformed human civilization.

Most people on Earth are not aware of the aliens' contributions to the science of para-theory, which has become an established and therefore normal science, in Kuhn's view. They believe that a scientist named Frederick Hallam is solely responsible, and in the first thirty years of this new science he has become the greatest and most revered scientist in history. Only one person, a bright young scientist named Peter Lamont, who is just beginning his career in para-theory, thinks that Hallam is a villain and a mediocrity. The first part of the novel is the story of Peter Lamont and the difficulties he faces in going against accepted scientific paradigms and human self-interest in the name of scientific truth. Lamont is writing a history of the science, and he soon finds that the existing literature on "the amazing story of the development of the Electron Pump" has been written in such a way as to obscure the useful contributions of many people other than Hallam—among them Benjamin Denison, the hero of the third part of the book.

Actually, Lamont's efforts to discredit Hallam are motivated by a desire for revenge. Hallam had refused to recognize the contributions of the aliens—the main subject of Lamont's Ph.D. thesis—and had branded Lamont's work "mysticism" (it must be pointed out that the exact means by which the aliens know about and communicate with our Universe does border on fantasy). This had damaged Lamont's career by plunging him into obscurity, and he is now determined to prove that Hallam and the science on which he arrogantly rests is wrong. Lamont therefore begins a intellectual quest that examines the assumptions, "the weak point in any theory," behind para-theory. What Lamont eventually discovers—with the help of cryptic messages about the danger of the Pump, sent by Dua, one of the Emotional aliens—is that the continued operation of the Pump will eventually cause the sun to become a nova, perhaps in the near future.

For technical reasons that are described in detail in the book, Lamont is unable to present incontrovertible proof of his theory to the authorities and is thus further discredited. The technological means to prove his theory are available on the moon, however, which now represents the cutting edge of science because thousands of the best scientists live there, enwombed in a world apart. They have developed an instrument called a Pionizer, which can detect incredibly small amounts of radiation. With this advance, Denison, another scientist cast into obscurity by Hallam, is able to prove that the rate of increase of intensity of strong nuclear interaction is what Lamont says it is, not what orthodox theory would have it be. Nor will Earth have to abandon its energy source. Through Denison's work with the Pionizer, the leaking of radiation from an anti-para-Universe is discovered. This energy, once humanity taps into it, will counteract the effects of the Electron Pump. In the end, Hallam is brought down, but the good name of science is saved.

Asimov has published works of juvenile science fiction—first in the Lucky Starr series, published in the 1950s under the pseudonym of Paul French—but they have not contributed much to his reputation. However, as new discoveries about the planets of our solar system have been made, Asimov has written prefaces for the books, which remain in print, updating the science and explaining inaccuracies in the stories—a practice that indicates his concern that he not misinform young readers. In *Lucky Starr and the Oceans of Venus* (1954), for example, Lucky must deal with a large sea monster that inhabits the oceans of Venus. With the flyby of *Mariner II* in 1962, however, it was learned that Venus is much to hot to have the worldwide ocean described in Asimov's book, which had been developed in accordance with the scientific knowledge of its day. Asimov duly notes the new astronomical facts in the preface. Actually, apart from any literary qualities the books may or may not have, this aspect—the encroachment of error into science-fiction narrative, which bases itself on connections with the real world as known by science—is by far the most interesting thing about them.

There are also the novels *Fantastic Voyage* (1966) and *Fantastic Voyage II* (1987). As Asimov explains in his autobiography, the first was a novelization of a motion picture that had been written by others (many erroneously assume the opposite and think Asimov wrote the novel on which the film was based). Except for insupportable scientific inconsistencies, Asimov followed the plot line of the film as closely as he could; as a result, he felt the book was never truly his. When asked to write another novel on the same theme—a miniaturized vessel with a crew that is inside a living human being—Asimov agreed on the condition that he be allowed to do it entirely his own way. *Fantastic Voyage II* is thus not really a sequel, although it uses some of the same science-fictional devices. This time the story takes place during the twenty-first century in the Soviet Union, where a top Soviet scientist, Pyotor Shapirov, lies deep in a coma, the victim of a miniaturization accident. A kidnapped American scientist named Albert Jonas Morrison and a team of four Soviet scientists travel to the dying Shapirov's brain in a specially designed submarine to save his life. Although Shapirov dies and the mission is apparently a failure, many laws governing the science of miniaturization are discovered. The American scientist realizes that he has found the exact neural mechanisms that control telepathy, but the Americans and the Soviets will have to cooperate in order to make practical use of the information.

Asimov's most recent novel, *Nemesis* (1989), is much more a novel of character than an adventure story or a piece of hard-core scientific extrapolation, although the effect of technological advances on human beings is an important aspect of the story. The story takes place in the mid-twenty-first century, when Earth is overcrowded, worn out, anarchical, and perceived as socially degenerate and disease-ridden by the people of the Settlements (Earth's one hundred space colonies). One of these colonies, Rotor, led by the megalomaniac Janus Pitt, has sworn to leave Earth and the solar system forever in quest of a newer, purer society, which he wants to keep secret from Earth. The inhabitants develop a "hyper-assistance" drive that will enable them to travel to a previously undiscovered nearby star called Nemesis, where they will be safe from the Earth's intrusions.

Pitt also knows that Nemesis is destined to pass through the vicinity of Earth's solar system in a few thousand years, destroying the Earth before it will be possible to evacuate everyone on it. Because of his fanatical hatred of Earth, however, he keeps this fact a secret. When the story opens, Rotor, the renegade space colony, has been in orbit around Nemesis for thirty years. Near Nemesis is the planet Erythro, which circles another, larger planet,

Megas, which is actually a brown dwarf star. Rotor has established a scientific research station on Erythro, but most of its inhabitants still live on Rotor—including the hero of the story, Marlene Fisher, a fifteen-year-old girl who seems to have strange mental abilities. She learns of the dire threat that Nemesis poses to Earth from her mother, the astronomer who discovered Nemesis, but she is prevented from warning Earth. It is Marlene who establishes mental contact with Erythro, which turns out to be a sentient planet interested in studying other minds. Erythro is occupied by innumerable prokaryote cells capable of photosynthesis. Individually they are as primitive as life can be above the virus level, but taken together they form an organism of enormous complexity.

A crisis arises when a spaceship from Earth arrives at Rotor, which is supposed to be hidden. In the years since Rotor's departure, Earth had developed the technology of superliminal flight and had managed to equip one ship with it. The representatives from Earth want to make a deal with Rotor. They too have discovered the danger posed to Earth by Nemesis, but until all humanity has true superliminal flight—in which case distance will no longer be a factor and human beings will search out not the nearest star but the most comfortable star—Erythro can be terraformed and used as a waystation. Earth has developed an evacuation program that should last several thousand years, one that will end with the necessary abandonment of Earth and the beginning of the colonization of the Galaxy. In exchange Earth will give Rotor the technology of superliminal flight so that the planet can maintain its secrecy.

Marlene is involved in these negotiations and speaks on behalf of Erythro. It seems that the organism that inhabits Erythro would be destroyed by terraforming. Marlene is instrumental in solving the crisis when she facilitates a mind link between Erythro's vast mind and a scientist from Earth. She also helps the scientist uncover the "hidden knowledge" he acquired during the contact by questioning him about "gravitational repulsion," an aspect of superluminal flight. It seems that asteroids in orbit around Nemesis could be made to shift in and out of hyperspace, creating a disturbance that would deflect the course of Nemesis enough to make it miss Earth's solar system.

As the novel ends, more scientists from Earth are planning to arrive and use Erythro's vast knowledge. Thus there is no longer any purpose to be served by Pitt's project of secretly building a new civilization. In fact, he now has to supervise the project for the salvation of Earth. Rotor is no longer hidden and can be reached at any time; Earth would turn against it if

Rotor did not rejoin the human race. Asimov makes it clear at the end that all of this could not have been accomplished without Marlene.

## Asimov's Reputation

Asimov has always been very popular with fans, who awarded him a Special Hugo Award in 1962 for his science articles in *Fantasy and Science Fiction* and another Hugo (Best All-Time Series) in 1966 for the Foundation series. In addition to these special awards, Asimov won both the Hugo and Nebula awards in 1973 for *The Gods Themselves*. When he made the *New York Times* bestseller list for the first time in 1982 with *Foundation's Edge,* the long-awaited sequel to the Foundation trilogy, the fans again awarded him a Hugo.

Asimov is credited with a number of innovations in the field of science fiction that helped to transform it away from the space opera adventures of the 1930s into a more intellectually responsible fiction. Certainly, his humanly engineered robots obeying the Three Laws of Robotics were a change from the mechanical monsters of the previous era. He seems also to have solidified the convention of a Galactic Empire—its rise, reign, and fall—which has been taken for granted in many millennia-spanning novels that came after his, including the famous Dune novels of Frank Herbert, and *Star Wars*.[3]

But science fiction is nothing if not a literature of change. One man's innovations often became the next man's accepted premises, and then may become stale and worn out. Critics such as Brian Aldiss have asserted that the presence of such giants as Asimov in the field distorts judgment of what is being done not merely by publishers but also by a number of young writers entering the genre. Aldiss believes that a kind of renaissance of Golden Age / Campbellian science fiction is going on, in which the "old dinosaurs"—Heinlein, Hubbard (who has published at least ten novels in the past few years), and Asimov—are beginning to dominate the field.[4] However, since the advent of cyberpunk and the deaths of both Hubbard and Heinlein, as well as of Frank Herbert, it is doubtful that this trend will continue.

Indeed, cyberpunk authors (such as Rudy Rucker, in his two books *Wetware* and *Software*) have attempted a revisionary swerve away from the Asimovian vision of robots as man's technological servants. Some robots in these novels have been freed of the "ugly, human-chauvinist priorities of Asimov" and have begun to evolve on their own. In fact, a revolution is going on, and the object of it is to create subversive programs that will outwit "Asimov behavior" in robots (i.e., behavior according to the Three Laws of Robotics). In Rucker's novels, robots who are not so freed are called "Asimov slaves" by the liberated ones, known as "boppers."[5] Since Rucker's vision is largely comic, satiric, and exaggerated, I am not sure how far this criticism is intended to go—but other cyberpunk writers, such as Bruce Sterling, have declared that they want to forget the Three Laws of Robotics.

Asimov's reaction to the newer writers and his own assessment of his status as a science-fiction superstar are quite frank:

> Well, you know, I'm a has-been. The stuff I write now is exactly what I wrote in the 1940s and 1950s, and we have people writing eighties stuff now, and that's what . . . the people who vote, vote for. It's very unlikely that I'll ever have a novel nominated again. I don't expect to. Fortunately, the readers are interested enough to buy the books, so that the fact that I don't get nominated . . . might fill my eyes with tears and makes it hard for me to make out my deposit slips . . . but I can do it! (1988 interview)

Few critical assessments of Asimov exist in which the whole extent of his imaginative universe is considered. James Gunn's study of Asimov, as well as Joseph Patrouch's, are outdated in their assumptions because they were written before Asimov decided to link the nonrobotic universe of the Foundation with the robot novels. And Brian Aldiss makes rather hasty and offhanded judgments when he labels Asimov's attempts at narrative continuity "a painful obsession," saying that they are "more ingenious than satisfactory, and more absurd than ingenious."[6] Actually, as I have tried to show in this study, Asimov has written a kind of "epic of knowledge" that legitimates two new sciences: robotics, a normal science, and psychohistory, an extraordinary one. The former follows the rules of a paradigm, the Three Laws of Robotics, that is never seriously questioned. The latter follows a more Popperian model in the sense that during the course of the novels it is "risked" in a series of crises of the Seldon Plan and is finally found inadequate. Yet psychohistory, if by that we mean we mean the notion of science as a steady accumulation of positive knowledge, never was a foundation for the series.

As early as the first novel of the classic trilogy, when we find out that the project of the Encyclopedia Galactica was only a ruse, we are led to question the notion of science being founded on anything other than a perpetual quest to prove itself wrong. By the time of the Mule it is clearly stated that psychohistory as the foundation of the Seldon Plan is not an absolute—it is "neither complete nor correct" but the best that could be done at the time.

The Seldon Plan is described as an "evolving mechanism." Absolutes, great final generalities of thought, are here rejected by Asimov as signs of a decaying culture. The later novels uncover the hidden assumptions underlying the laws of psychohistory, in effect laying bare the unthought premises from which the story of the Foundation series was generated.

This later narrative work I would characterize as novelistic, as opposed to epic, for the following reasons. Patrick Parrinder points out that the science-fiction epic has for the most part suffered from truncation or frustration because its basis is not history but speculation or prophecy, and it invokes the authority of the modern cognitive sciences for its speculations about the far future: "If the events they portray are of epic magnitude, the manner of their portrayal is brief and allegorical . . . reminiscent of fables."[7] It is certainly true that Asimov's early stories display these characteristics. They leap from decade to decade and from social group to social group without ever giving us a strong central character or convincing details. Indeed, the central contradiction of Asimov's work lies in the contrast between its scientific up-to-dateness (there are references to chaos theory as the model for psychohistory in *Prelude to Foundation,* as opposed to references to the kinetic theory of gases in the classic Foundation novels) and the extreme anachronism inherent in his characterizations and literary style, which are based on those of nineteenth-century British popular novels and fit oddly in the context of a galactic empire.

Yet all this may be due in part to the fact that much of his work was originally published as short stories and novellas for pulp science-fiction magazines. Although Asimov proclaims that his style has not changed in the intervening years, the later novels are more complex in terms of narrative. *Foundation and Earth* reads like an equation in three unknowns: the location and fate of the Earth, why Trevize chooses Galaxia, and what has happened to the robots are all interrelated mysteries in the narrative. It is much to Asimov's credit that he does not let this complex narrative to degenerate into chaos or allow the secrets to interfere unduly with our orderly comprehension of it. His characters, or at least the main ones, are also more open-ended. They are less formulated than earlier characters who seem to act out their lives in an epically distanced past.

It is significant, I think, that in the most recent novels (with the exception of *Prelude to Foundation,* where they seem appropriate) Asimov drops the quotations from the Encyclopedia Galactica that usually opened chapters and that referred to the characters as if they were already dead ("finalized"). Golan Trevize, the hero and central focus of *Foundation's Edge* and *Foundation and Earth,* has a much more direct contact with the present as he searches for the reasons behind his intuitive choice of Galaxia for the future of mankind. His is a consciousness that lives on in its unfinalizedness. Asimov even stresses that Trevize's mind has "gaps" in it and that he is capable of doing unforeseen and surprising things. We are not yet in a novelistic world as richly detailed as Frank Herbert's Dune series, to which Asimov's work is often compared; nevertheless, the differences in the later novels are evidence of Asimov's evolution as a writer.

Considered as whole, Asimov's imaginative universe has contributed much to the speculative wealth of science fiction. In the spirit of critical rationalism, he presents us with the adventures of two invented sciences, robotics and psychohistory, which develop through the testing and questioning of the assumptions on which they were founded. Asimov's universe is therefore a superior one in terms of the qualities characteristic of science fiction as a literature of ideas.

# *Appendix*
# Main Characters in the Asimovian Universe

### *The End of Eternity*

Andrew Harlan: protagonist; Technician; destroyer of Eternity.
Hobbe Finge: Harlan's antagonist; Senior Computer in the 482nd century.
Laban Twissell: Senior Computer; an important member of the Allwhen Council who tries to save Eternity.
Brinsley Sheridan Cooper: a young man interested in Primitive History.
Nöys Lambert: Finge's secretary; Harlan's love interest.
Vikkor Mallansohn: builder of the Temporal Field, which makes Eternity possible.

### *I, Robot*

Susan Calvin: chief robopsychologist at U.S. Robots.
Gregory Powell and Mike Donovan: a pair of engineers who field-test robots.
Stephen Byerley: district attorney; later the first World Co-ordinator; a robot.
Robbie, Dave, Cutie, Speedy, and Herbie: various models of robots created by U.S. Robots.

### *The Caves of Steel*

Elijah Baley: protagonist; Earth detective.
R. Daneel Olivaw: an Auroran humaniform robot; Baley's partner.
Dr. Roj Nemennuh Sarton: an Auroran scientist; the creator of Daneel in his own image; the murder victim.
Dr. Han Fastolfe: Aurora's greatest theoretical robotocist; an advocate of C/Fe culture.
Commissioner Julius Enderby: Baley's boss; a Medievalist; and the murderer.

### *The Naked Sun*

Elijah Baley, R. Daneel Olivaw.
Rikaine Delmarre: a Solarian fetal engineer; the murder victim.
Gladia Delmarre: Rikaine's wife, accused of his murder.

Hannis Gruer: head of Solarian security.
Jothan Leebig: a roboticist; close friend of the Delmarres; the murderer.
Anselmo Quemot, a sociologist; Klorissa Cantoro, Delmarre's female lab assistant; and Dr. Altim Thool, a physician and Gladia's genetic father: all murder suspects.

### *The Robots of Dawn*

Elijah Baley, R. Daneel Olivaw, Han Fastolfe, Gladia Solaria (formerly Gladia Delmarre).
Jander Panell: a humaniform robot created by Fastolfe and given to Gladia; the murder victim.
Giskard Reventlov: another (accidentally telepathic) robot created by Fastolfe; the real murderer.
Vasilia Aliena: Fastolfe's genetic daughter.
Santirix Gremionis: a personnel artist; a murder suspect.
Kelden Amadiro: Director of the Robotics Institute; Fastolfe's opponent; the apparent murderer.

### *Robots and Empire*

R. Daneel Olivaw, Giskard Reventlov, Elijah Baley (in flashback), Gladia Solaria, Kelden Amadiro, Vasilia Aliena, Han Fastolfe.
Daneel Giskard Baley: a Trader; seventh-generation descendant of Elijah Baley.
Levular Mandamus: an ambitious young scientist at the Robotics Institute; inventor of the plot to destroy Earth.

### *The Stars, Like Dust*

Sander Jonti: villain; a Tyranni; Autarch of Lingane.
The Rancher of Widemos: a murdered leader of the resistance.
Biron Farrill: protagonist; the Rancher's son.
Hinrik: Director of Rhodia; a secret supporter of the rebellion.
Artemisia: Hinrik's daughter; Farrill's love interest.
Gillbret: Artemisia's uncle; a supporter of the rebellion.
Commissioner Simok Aratap of Tyrann: must locate the rebellion world.

### *The Currents of Space*

Rik: an Earthman, a Spatio-analyst whose memory has been destroyed.
Valona March: a Florinian peasant girl assigned to care for Rik.

Myrlyn Terens: a Florinian educated on Sark for the civil service; destroyer of Rik's memory.
The Squire of Fife: an absentee landlord blackmailed by Terens.
Ludigan Abel: the Trantorian Ambassador to Sark.
Dr. Selim Junz: a Spatio-analyst investigating Rik's disappearance.

### *Pebble in the Sky*

Joseph Schwartz: a sixty-two-year-old retired tailor, transported to Earth's far future; protagonist.
Bel Arvardan: a distinguished young archeologist investigating mankind's origins.
Affret Shekt: inventor of the Synapsifier.
Pola Shekt: Affret's daughter; Avardan's love interest.
Ennius: Procurator of Earth.
Balkis: Secretary to the High Minister of Earth; plots to destroy the Trantorian Empire.

### *Prelude to Foundation*

Hari Seldon: mathematician; founder of psychohistory.
Cleon I: the Trantorian Emperor.
Eto Demerzel: Cleon's Chief of Staff (actually R. Daneel Olivaw).
Chetter Hummin: a journalist (actually R. Daneel Olivaw).
Dors Venabili: a woman historian; Seldon's love interest.
Mayor of Wye: a political rival of Cleon's.
Mother Rittah: an inhabitant of Trantor's slums who knows the myths of Earth.
Davan: a popular rebel leader.

### *Foundation*

Hari Seldon (as a simulacrum).
Salvor Hardin: Mayor of Terminus; defeats Anacreon.
Leopold: King of Anacreon.
Wienis: the Prince Regent, Leopold's uncle.
Sef Sermak: Hardin's rival in the City Council.
Limmar Ponyets: a Trader.
Hober Mallow: first of the Merchant Princes.

### *Foundation and Empire*

Hari Seldon (as a simulacrum).
Bel Riose: an ambitious and capable general of the Empire.

Ducem Barr: a noble; expert on Foundation lore.
Cleon II: the Trantorian Emperor.
Brodrig: sent by Cleon to investigate Riose.
Lathan Devers: a young Trader; agent for the Foundation.
The Mule: a mutant bent on conquering the Empire.
Magnifico: his Fool (actually the Mule in disguise).
Bayta Darell: a Foundation citizen; the Mule's love object.
Ebling Mis: a Foundation scientist searching for the Second Foundation; killed by Bayta.
Han Pritcher: a Foundation spy; later converted by the Mule.

### *Second Foundation*

The Mule, Han Pritcher.
Bail Channis: an unconverted citizen of Terminus; sent out by the Mule to find the Second Foundation.
Dr. Toran Darell: leader of a group of conspirators.
Arkady Darell: Toran's teenage daughter; Bayta's granddaughter; converted by the Second Foundation.
Homir Munn: a librarian; conspirator; sent to Kalgan to find the Second Foundation.
Lord Stettin: ruler of Kalgan; attacks Foundation.
Pelleas Anthor: an agent of the Second Foundation.
Preem Palver: the First Speaker of the Second Foundation.

### *Foundation's Edge*

Hari Seldon (as a simulacrum).
Harla Branno: tough, pragmatic Mayor of Terminus.
Golan Trevize: protagonist; a Councilman of Terminus.
Munn Li Compor: Trevize's fellow Councilman; an agent of the Second Foundation.
Janov Pelorat: historian who studies Earth's myths.
Stor Gendibal: next in line to be First Speaker.
Delora Delarmi: Gendibal's political rival.
Sura Novi: Gendibal's female companion; a Gaian agent.
Bliss: spokeswoman for the planet Gaia.
Dom: a Gaian elder who tells myths of origins.

### *Foundation and Earth*

Bliss, Trevize, Pelorat, R. Daneel Olivaw.
Mitza Lizalor: Comporellian Minister of Transportation; has an affair with Trevize.
Dr. Deniador: a Comporellian Skeptic who knows myths of Earth.
Sarton Bander: a Solarian, killed by Bliss.
Fallom: a hermaphroditic Solarian child.
Hiroko: an Alphan girl who infects Trevize.

# *Notes and References*

*Preface*

1. Gerard Genette, *Narrative Discourse: An Essay in Method,* trans. Jane E. Lewin (Ithaca, N.Y.: Cornell University Press, 1980).

2. Thomas Kuhn, *The Structure of Scientific Revolutions* (Chicago: University of Chicago Press, 1970).

3. Brian Aldiss, *Trillion-Year Spree* (New York: Avon Books, 1986), 264.

*Chapter One*

1. Isaac Asimov, letter to author, 14 May 1988.

2. Charles Platt, *Dream Makers* (New York: Berkley Books, 1980), 6.

3. Stefan Kanfer, "The Protean Penman," *Time,* 19 December 1988, 80–82.

4. Isaac Asimov, Afterword to *The Alternate Asimovs* (New York: Signet Books, 1986), 313.

5. Isaac Asimov, *Asimov's New Guide to Science* (New York: Basic Books, 1984), 780.

6. "Isaac Asimov Speaks: The PBS Interviews," *Humanist* (January / February 1989):5–13.

7. Isaac Asimov, *Asimov's Galaxy: Reflections on Science Fiction* (New York: Doubleday, 1989), 175.

8. Donald M. Hassler, "Some Asimovian Resonances from the Enlightenment," *Science Fiction Studies* 15, part 1 (March 1988):36–47.

9. The controversy surrounding Asimov's public persona as a sensuous "dirty old man" and self-satisfied genius recently had a hilarious public airing in *Asimov's Science Fiction Magazine.* In two texts he does refer to "sedulously cultivating" a persona (*In Joy Still Felt* [New York: Avon Books, 1980], 106; *Asimov on Science Fiction* [New York: Doubleday, 1981], 224).

10. Isaac Asimov, interview with the author, 5 July 1988. (Subsequent uses of this material identified in text.)

11. Asimov, *In Joy Still Felt,* 180.

12. See Asimov, *Asimov's Galaxy,* 392–95.

13. Isaac Asimov, *In Memory Yet Green* (New York: Doubleday, 1979), 89.

14. Ibid., 90.

15. My understanding of how this effect of scientific knowledge is created in Asimovian narrative is based on my reading of Jean-Francois Lyotard's *The Postmodern Condition: A Report on Knowledge,* vol. 10 of *Theory and History of Litera-*

*ture,* trans. Geoff Bennington and Brian Massumi (Minneapolis: University of Minnesota Press, 1984). By and large, Lyotard's report is an investigation of the role that narrative structures play in legitimating science. He distinguishes broadly between two aspects of this legitimation process: a first-order "natural" narrative (which Lyotard terms "narrative knowledge" or "popular narrative pragmatics") and a higher plane of understanding, on which the story would yield its true significance. This second level always invokes some higher, metanarrative authority, some "large scale explanatory program," such as the dialectic of Enlightenment, the notion of progress, or the emancipation of the working subject in Marxism.

The main difference between the two levels of narrative lies in how they treat legitimation. According to Lyotard, narrative knowledge does not give priority to the question of its own legitimation. Rather, "it certifies itself in the pragmatics of its own transmission, without having recourse to argumentation and proof" (p. 27). It is largely equated with the situation of the storyteller in a traditional society (cf. such Asimovian characters as Mother Rittah in *Prelude to Foundation,* who knows the legends and myths of the Earth; see chapter 6). Mother Rittah knows the stories she tells are true *because* she can recount them. On the other hand, metanarratives (such as the Seldon Plan) have to legitimate themselves by making reference to a logic of scientific discovery that involves the verification of a paradigm (Thomas Kuhn) or the falsification of a theory (Karl Popper). The ideas of both Kuhn and Popper and their relation to Asimovian narrative are discussed in chapter 2.

For Lyotard, science desires its statements to be true but does not have the resources to legitimate their truth on its own. Hence its recourse, in the public political domain, to "epics of knowledge" to legitimate itself: "The state spends large amounts of money to enable science to pass itself off as an epic: the State's own credibility is based on that epic, which it uses to obtain the public consent its decision makers need" (p. 28). One has only to think of NASA's politics of legitimating the space program to realize that Lyotard is very discerning in this matter.

As a science popularizer, Asimov has been deeply implicated in the legitimation of science. An entire book could be written on the impact of his nonfiction works in the public domain and the narrative structures they employ. In this book I consider only the formal relation of Asimov's fiction to the epic (see chapter 7).

*Chapter Two*

1. Isaac Asimov, *The Alternate Asimovs* (New York: Doubleday, 1986), 169–254.

2. For a discussion of the time loop, see Stanislaw Lem, "The Time-Travel Story and Related Matters of SF Structuring," *Science Fiction Studies* 1, no. 3 (Spring 1974): 143–54.

3. For an introduction to narratology, see Seymour Chatman, *Story and Discourse: Narrative Structure in Fiction and Film* (Ithaca, N.Y.: Cornell University Press, 1978).

4. In explaining these concepts, I have relied heavily on Gerard Genette,

*Narrative Discourse: An Essay in Method,* trans. Jane E. Lewin (Ithaca, N.Y.: Cornell University Press, 1980), 33–85 and throughout.

5. Isaac Asimov, *Nine Tomorrows* (New York: Doubleday, 1959), 189.

6. As Asimov describes it, the process of professional initiation into the scientific society of the Eternals—which consists of learning paradigms and rules of research and behavior—comes very close to initiation into normal science, as that practice is conceived by Thomas S. Kuhn in *The Structure of Scientific Revolutions* (Chicago: University of Chicago Press, 1970). According to Kuhn, normal science occurs when a community acquires a paradigm that structures the kinds of problems scientists recognize as legitimate for investigation and that also guarantees the existence of a stable solution to those problems. It is predicated on the assumption that the scientific community knows what the world is like. Furthermore, normal science often suppresses fundamental novelties because they are subversive to its basic commitments, which are in the main dedicated to refining and articulating the points of contact between the theory that the paradigm supplies and nature. It does not aim at calling forth new sorts of phenomena or at inventing new theories to account for those phenomena.

Most importantly for Kuhn, however, normal science is akin to puzzle solving or problem solving because it provides rules that tell the practitioner of a science what both the world and his science are like. Knowing this—implictly in the form of a paradigm or explicitly in the form of rules—he can concentrate with assurance on the problems that these rules and existing knowledge define for him. As Kuhn somewhat disparagingly characterizes it, normal science is a kind of "mopping-up operation," but one not without challenges for a certain type of scientific personality. The challenges of normal science lie in the area of skills, in finding an ingenious solution to a puzzle. In *The End of Eternity* Andrew Harlan is depicted as a highly skilled Observer but no more than that.

Since many of Asimov's stories, particularly the robot stories, test our ingenuity or skill in solving a problem with a guaranteed solution (e.g., a solution that does not invalidate the Three Laws of Robotics), it would not be an exaggeration to say that the typical Asimovian story operates within the parameters of normal science. The narrative that defines normal science is one in which scientific knowledge must have a foundation in past scientific achievements. As Kuhn explains, normal science is written in a cumulative yet piecemeal process, in which items are added, "singly and in combination, to the ever growing stockpile that constitutes scientific technique and knowledge. And history of science becomes the discipline that chronicles both these successive increments and the obstacles that have inhibited their accumulation" (p. 2). This concept of development by accumulation governs almost all of Asimov's popularizations of science. Lyotard would recognize in these books the operation of one of the two "Master Narratives" that legitimate science: totalization, or the idea that the goal of science is the amassing of the totality of knowledge (the other is the dialectic of Englightenment—that knowledge is the necessary precondition for liberation). (See note 15 to Chapter 1.)

On the other hand, Kuhn sees the writing of the history of science as an anachronistic process in which the acquistion of a paradigm retrospectively reconfigures the entire field of scientific investigation (p. 35). Thus Asimov's fondness for plotting his works through such a process and for writing stories with puzzle characteristics may have more to do with the research tradition in which he was trained at Columbia University than with any influence of science fiction.

When Asimov made his first major statement about the nature of science-fiction narrative ("Social Science Fiction," in *Modern Science Fiction,* ed. Reginald Bretnor New York: Coward-McCann, 1953), he elaborated on a chess analogy to explain how he devised his own stories, especially the Foundation stories. He also used this analogy to examine the work of other science-fiction authors. What emerges from the essay is a sense of science fiction as a rule-bound extrapolation of the effects of technological change on society. Interestingly, Kuhn often describes the research worker in normal science as a solver of puzzles, not as someone who questions the rules of the game supplied by the paradigm; he compares the researcher to a chess player confronted with a chess problem (Kuhn, 38, 144). Many of Asimov's stories, especially the robot stories, seem to take place in a research tradition characterized by puzzle solving (see chapter 3).

Incidentally, I am not suggesting that Asimov is unaware of other modes of writing the history of science or of writing science-fiction; indeed, there is evidence to the contrary. For instance, he contributed a foreward to a festschrift for Karl Popper in 1982, so he could hardly be unaware of a view of science radically opposed to the idea that sciences are bodies of established fact.

7. Isaac Asimov, *The End of Eternity,* in *The Far Ends of Time and Earth,* vol. 1 of *The Collected Fiction of Isaac Asimov* (New York: Doubleday, 1979), 519.

8. Ibid., 537.

9. Genette, *Narrative Discourse,* 35.

10. Isaac Asimov, Introduction to *Far Ends of Time and Earth,* xiv.

11. Damon Knight, *In Search of Wonder* (Chicago: Advent Publishers, 1967), 94.

12. Joseph Patrouch, Jr., *The Science Fiction of Isaac Asimov* (New York: Doubleday, 1974), 145.

13. James Gunn, *Isaac Asimov: The Foundations of Science Fiction* (Oxford: Oxford University Press, 1982), 183–84.

14. Karl Popper, *Conjectures and Refutations: The Growth of Scientific Knowledge* (New York: Harper and Row, 1968), 26, 36–37.

15. Isaac Asimov, "A Literature of Ideas," in *Today and Tomorrow* (New York: Dell Books, 1973), 305–13.

*Chapter Three*

1. See Asimov's Introduction to *Robot Dreams* (New York: Berkley Books, 1986), 7.

2. Asimov most recently expressed this view in an essay entitled "The Little Tin God of Characterization," *Asimov's SF Magazine*, May 1985, 25–37.

3. Thomas Kuhn, *The Structure of Scientific Revolutions* (Chicago: University of Chicago Press, 1970), 136.

4. Isaac Asimov, *The Rest of the Robots* (New York: Pyramid Books, 1966), 51.

5. Kuhn, *Structure of Scientific Revolutions,* 27.

6. Isaac Asimov, *I, Robot* (New York: Signet Books, 1956), 61.

7. Kuhn, *Structure of Scientific Revolutions,* 148.

8. Ibid., 169.

9. See A. J. Greimas and J. Courtes, "The Cognitive Dimension of Narrative Discourse," *New Literary History* 7, no. 3, (1976): 433–37.

10. Asimov, *Rest of the Robots,* 87.

11. Kuhn specifies three classes of anomalies in *The Structure of Scientific Revolutions* (96–97).

*Chapter Four*

1. John G. Cawelti, *Adventure, Mystery, and Romance* (Chicago: University of Chicago Press, 1976), 137.

2. Ibid., 81–82.

3. James Gunn, *Isaac Asimov, The Foundations of Science Fiction* (Oxford: Oxford University Press, 1982), 127.

*Chapter Five*

1. Isaac Asimov, *Prisoners of the Stars: The Collected Fiction of Isaac Asimov,* vol. 2 (New York: Doubleday, 1979), xii.

2. Joseph F. Patrouch, Jr., *The Science Fiction of Isaac Asimov* (New York: Doubleday, 1974), 133–34.

3. Ibid., 123–25.

*Chapter Six*

1. Thomas Kuhn, *The Structure of Scientific Revolutions* (Chicago: The University of Chicago Press, 1970), 86–87, 163.

2. I leave it to the experts to determine whether psychohistory in Asimov is supposed to represent the science that Marxism never became, as some critics have maintained, or whether a true science of social prediction is even possible. For an attempt at working out a theory of psychohistory, see Michael F. Flynn's "An Introduction to Psychohistory" in *Analog* (April 1988): 60–78, and *Analog* (May 1988): 38–64.

3. For an account of the novum and how it functions in science-fiction narrative, see Darko Suvin, *Metamorphoses of Science Fiction* (New Haven: Yale University Press, 1979), 63–84.

*Chapter Seven*

1. Joseph F. Patrouch, Jr., *The Science Fiction of Isaac Asimov* (New York: Doubleday, 1974), 183–252.

2. James Gunn, *Isaac Asimov: The Foundations of Science Fiction* (Oxford: Oxford University Press, 1982), 215.

3. See the discussion in Donald A. Wollheim, *The Universe Makers* (New York: Harper and Row, 1971), 37–41.

4. Brian Aldiss, *Trillion-Year Spree* (New York: Avon Books, 1986), 384.

5. Rudy Rucker, *Software* (New York: Avon Books, 1982), 53; *Wetware* (New York: Avon Books, 1988), 97.

6. Aldiss, 391.

7. Patrick Parrinder, *Science Fiction: Its Criticism and Teaching* (New York: Methuen, 1980), 93. Actually, since the classic Foundation series clearly suggests the rise and fall of the roman empire as a historical parallel for understanding events in it, and since psychohistory seems to predict the future based on a study of the past, Asimov has often been accused of historical determinism, or a version of what Karl Popper calls "the poverty of historicism." In historicism, history is idolized because of a fear of freedom and a lack of openness to the future. It has to be admitted that some of these early stories (particularly "The Dead Hand," *Astounding,* April 1945, now chapter 3 of *Foundation and Empire,* a story apparently influenced by Toynbee) do show humans in the grip of historical necessity. Even so, in these early stories what seems to interest Asimov most is the interplay of free will and determinism. As I have been at pains to point out, the later novels discard the Seldon Plan, and with it the notion that human history if predictable, or even entirely rational.

# *Selected Bibliography*

PRIMARY SOURCES

*Fiction*

Unless otherwise noted, the works listed are novels.

*The Alternate Asimovs.* New York: Doubleday, 1986 (novellas).
*The Caves of Steel.* New York: Doubleday, 1954.
*The Currents of Space.* New York: Doubleday, 1952.
*The End of Eternity.* New York: Doubleday, 1955.
*Fantastic Voyage.* New York: Houghton Mifflin, 1966.
*Fantastic Voyage II.* New York: Doubleday, 1987.
*Foundation.* New York: Gnome Press, 1951.
*Foundation and Earth.* New York: Doubleday, 1986.
*Foundation and Empire.* New York: Gnome Press, 1952.
*Foundation's Edge.* New York: Doubleday, 1982.
*The Gods Themselves.* New York: Doubleday, 1972.
*I, Robot.* New York: Gnome Press, 1950 (short-story cycle).
*Lucky Star and the Oceans of Venus.* New York: Doubleday, 1954 (juvenile).
*The Naked Sun.* New York: Doubleday, 1957.
*Nemesis.* New York: Doubleday, 1989.
*Nightfall and Other Stories.* New York: Doubleday, 1969 (stories).
*Nine Tomorrows.* New York: Doubleday, 1959 (stories).
*Pebble in the Sky.* New York: Doubleday, 1950.
*Prelude to Foundation.* New York: Doubleday, 1988.
*The Rest of the Robots.* New York: Doubleday, 1964 (stories).
*Robot Dreams.* New York: Berkley, 1986 (stories).
*Robots and Empire.* New York: Doubleday, 1985.
*The Robots of Dawn.* New York: Doubleday, 1983.
*Second Foundation.* New York: Gnome Press, 1953.
*The Stars, Like Dust.* New York: Doubleday, 1951.

*Nonfiction*

***Books***

*Asimov on Science Fiction.* New York: Doubleday, 1981 (essays).

*Asimov's Galaxy: Reflections on Science Fiction.* New York: Doubleday, 1989 (essays).

*Asimov's New Guide to Science.* New York: Basic Books, 1984.

*In Joy Still Felt.* New York: Doubleday, 1980 (autobiography).

*In Memory Yet Green.* New York: Doubleday, 1979 (autobiography).

### *Essays and Interviews*

"Isaac Asimov." In *Dream Makers: Interviews by Charles Platt.* New York: Berkley, 1980.

"Isaac Asimov Speaks: The PBS Interviews." *Humanist* (January/February 1989): 5–13.

"The Little Tin God of Characterization." *Asimov's Science Fiction Magazine* 9, no. 5 (May 1985): 25–37.

"A Literature of Ideas." In *Today and Tomorrow.* New York: Dell Books, 1973, 305–13.

## SECONDARY SOURCES

### *Books and Parts of Books*

**Aldiss, Brian W.** *Trillion Year Spree: The History of Science Fiction.* New York: Avon, 1986. A literary history of science fiction that discusses Asimov in relation to the norms of Campbellian science fiction.

**Gunn, James.** *Isaac Asimov: The Foundations of Science Fiction.* Oxford: Oxford University Press, 1982. Stoutly defends Asimov against his detractors with an approach called "criticism in context," which places emphasis on the conditions under which the work was written and published.

**Knight, Damon.** "Asimov and Empire." In *In Search of Wonder.* Chicago: Advent Publishers, 1967, 90–94.

**Olander, Joseph D.,** and **Martin H. Greenberg,** eds. *Isaac Asimov.* New York: Taplinger, 1977. Brings together a variety of essays on Asimov, concluding with Asimov's response to the analyses.

**Patrouch, Joseph F., Jr.** *The Science Fiction of Isaac Asimov.* New York: Doubleday, 1974. A critical examination of Asimov's narrative style and techniques, using a traditional approach to literary criticism. Good discussions of Asimov's early work and story collections.

**Wollheim, Donald A.** "The Decline and Fall of the Galactic Empire." In *The Universe Makers.* New York: Harper & Row, 1971. Discusses how science fiction writers build upon conventions and how Asimov solidified the conventions of the Galactic Empire.

*Journal and Magazine Articles*

**Hassler, Donald M.** "Science Fiction and High Art." *Extrapolation* 28, no. 2 (Summer 1987): 187–93.

———. "Some Asimovian Resonances from the Enlightenment." *Science Fiction Studies* 15, part. 1 (March 1988): 36–47.

**Ingersoll, Earl G.,** ed. "A Conversation With Isaac Asimov." *Science Fiction Studies* 14, part. 1 (March 1987): 68–77.

**Kanfer, Stephen.** "The Protean Penman." *Time,* 19 December 1988, 80–82.

**Lem, Stanislaw.** "The Time-Travel Story and Related Matters of SF Structuring." *Science Fiction Studies* 1, no. 3 (Spring 1974): 143–54.

# Index

## *The Author*

William F. Touponce received his Ph.D. in comparative literature from the University of Massachusetts, Amherst. He is now associate professor of English at Indiana University, Indianapolis, where he teaches children's literature, science fiction, and literary theory. He is the author of several books on fantasy and science-fiction authors, including Ray Bradbury and Frank Herbert, the latter in the Twayne series. He is currently at work on a study of postmodern science fiction.

## *The Editor*

Warren French (Ph.D., University of Texas, Austin) retired from Indiana University in 1986 and is now an honorary professor associated with the Board of American Studies at the University College of Swansea, Wales. In 1985 Ohio University awarded him a Doctor of Humane Letters degree. The editor of the contemporary (1945–75) titles in Twayne's United States Authors Series, he has contributed volumes on Jack Kerouac, Frank Norris, John Steinbeck, and J. D. Salinger. His most recent publication for Twayne is *The San Francisco Poetry Renaissance, 1955–1960.*